ESPRESSIVO

ESPRESSIVO

MUSIC AND LIFE

AT MARLBORO

Edited by J.M. Snyder

MARLBORO MUSIC SCHOOL AND FESTIVAL

Copyright © 1994 by Marlboro School of Music, Inc.
Published by Marlboro Music School and Festival, Marlboro, VT 05344
Library of Congress Catalog Card Number: 94-75877
Hardcover ISBN 0-9641014-0-8
Paperback ISBN 0-9641014-1-6

Designed by Jackie Schuman
Printed in the United States of America

FACING PAGE: *(Top)* Marcel Moyse. *(Bottom left)* Adolf Busch. *(Bottom right)* Irene Busch Serkin, Rudolf Serkin.

Espressivo: Music and Life at Marlboro celebrates the first four decades of the Marlboro Music School and Festival and the special spirit that permeates this unique musical community. It is dedicated to the memory of Rudolf Serkin, who for so many years provided generations of young musicians with the inspiration to strive for the highest artistic standards.

This publication was also created in tribute to Marlboro's other co-founders—Adolf and Herman Busch, and Marcel, Blanche and Louis Moyse; and with gratitude to Marlboro's many musicians, patrons and friends for their vital role in making the Marlboro ideal a reality. We also offer heartfelt thanks to those many photographers and writers whose images and words tell the story of Marlboro Music so movingly on these pages.

CONTENTS

The photographs in *Espressivo* are accompanied by the
insights of the musicians, journalists and publications listed above.

INTRODUCTION

Unlike Any Place in the World

What began as a musical experiment in the foothills of Vermont in 1951 is now widely recognized as the only institution of its kind—a retreat where exceptional young professional musicians gain invaluable artistic insights within the context of a closely knit family atmosphere. Marlboro Music is known throughout the world for igniting the explosion of interest in chamber music in this country over the past four decades and for providing a program and environment that have redefined standards for music preparation and performance.

It is the music, rather than the performance or the performers, that is the primary focus at Marlboro. In a location and atmosphere far removed from ordinary concert life, where music is viewed more as a passion than a profession, Marlboro participants explore works of their own choosing with unlimited rehearsal time and no obligation to perform for the simple, if elusive, purpose of achieving deeper artistic understanding and expression.

Central to the Marlboro philosophy is the belief that an openness and life-long dedication to continual learning is necessary in order to truly serve music. In a practice initiated by Marlboro, especially talented musicians at the beginning of their professional careers play side-by-side with master artists as equal participants. Through the intensive concentration on chamber music, that most democratic of musical forms, invaluable artistic insights and performance practices are passed down directly to those who aspire one day to become musical leaders in their own right.

A True Sense of Community

It was the violinist Adolf Busch who, upon settling with his family in rural southern Vermont in the 1940's, had the vision for such an experiment. It would be a relatively small community of professional musicians from throughout the world, of widely diverse ages and backgrounds. Taking time from their busy concert schedules, they would gather to share experiences and ideas not only in the daily rehearsals, but through living together, with their spouses and children, as one large family. The musicians would attend not for acclaim or financial reward, but to develop themselves as artists, united in their quest for the highest musical standards.

Adolf Busch, with his brother Herman, son-in-law Rudolf Serkin, and colleagues Marcel, Blanche and Louis Moyse, brought this dream to life by together founding the Marlboro Music School and Festival in Marlboro, Vermont. After Adolf Busch's sudden and untimely death in 1952, Rudolf Serkin carried on Marlboro's founding principles as its Artistic Director until his own passing in 1991. For over four decades, as this unusual musical community formed anew each season, Serkin dedicated himself tirelessly to Marlboro, touching and enriching the lives of its growing family and enthusiastic audiences with his unique spirit, artistry and intellect.

An Enduring Ideal

To this day, Marlboro Music remains deeply committed to the ideals of Busch, Serkin and the other founders. For seven weeks each summer, some 70 of the world's most talented professional musicians come together to rehearse, in great depth and with a minimum of distractions, works from the vast chamber music literature involving winds, voice, piano and strings. The participants, regardless of age, continue to be at once both students and teachers of music—colleagues searching together for the essence of artistic expression that lies beneath the printed notes.

Since the first summer, when the rehearsals and concerts were held in the converted barns and farm buildings of the newly-established Marlboro College, more than 1,400 musicians have participated at Marlboro. The participants have included musicians, who were selected primarily by audition, from throughout North and South America, and from many countries around the world including Australia, Austria, China, Czechoslovakia, England, France, Germany, Iceland, Israel, Italy, Japan, Korea, the Philippines, Russia and more.

At Marlboro, generations of musicians continue to live together with their families, sharing meals, social outings, chores and community activities. What remains at the heart of the Marlboro Music experience is a sense of spontaneity, generosity and informality—the willingness to take chances, to make mistakes, and to learn. It is a community whose members are committed to the belief that the finest in the art of music arises from that which is best in the human spirit.

Sharing the Marlboro Experience

Marlboro artists, both past and present, have shared the results of their experiences in this advanced study center with musicians and audiences throughout the world. Some who attended early in their careers and who have developed into today's musical leaders have returned to Marlboro as senior participants, offering to new generations what they themselves received decades ago. Many others have also contributed to a greatly expanded interest in the rich and ever-growing chamber music literature by founding important new series, festivals and educational programs that focus on this repertoire.

Marlboro participants can now be found as members of many of the most respected chamber ensembles of our time, some of which—including the Guarneri, Cleveland and Vermeer String Quartets—formed directly as a result of Marlboro. Other ensembles featuring Marlboro artists include string quartets such as the Emerson, Galimir, Juilliard, Mendelssohn, Muir and Orion; piano trios such as the Beaux Arts, Kalichstein-Laredo-Robinson, Mannes and Trio di Milano; ensembles such as Orpheus, St. Luke's and TASHI; and a considerable number of fine younger groups.

Former participants can also be counted among today's leading teachers at prominent international conservatories, colleges and universities. Still others are acclaimed concert soloists and recording artists, or members of symphony, opera and ballet orchestras in the United States and abroad. At the time of this writing, America's five major orchestras—Boston, Chicago, Cleveland, New York and Philadelphia—each count among their members between eight and twenty former Marlboro participants, many of whom are in principal chair positions.

In these and virtually all other areas of today's musical life, generations of past participants are paying tribute to the special legacy and ideals of Marlboro's founders. They are sharing with so many others the unique musical and human experiences, and the sense of joy inherent in making music, which they gained on a small hilltop in Vermont, in an experiment which has endured.

FACING PAGE: Marcel Moyse, Blanche Moyse, Louis Moyse.

THE FOUNDING,
THE EARLY YEARS,
THE CONCEPT

Just Making Music

"Just making music" is the way Rudolf Serkin expresses the main purpose of the Marlboro School of Music, which on July 1 will open a session of seven weeks at the college on Potash Hill.

Thirty-odd "students" have enrolled for the school but the term may be misleading. They are all advanced pupils or professional musicians and include several first-stand players from major eastern symphony orchestras.

Mr. Serkin emphasizes that the school will be strictly informal and that the top-flight artists will have no titles.

The primary music–making aim of the school can be broken down a little more, Mr. Serkin said. It will provide a rare opportunity for the attending musicians to do ensemble playing under ideal conditions and with almost every conceivable combination of instruments. Pianists and players of stringed instruments, woodwinds and brasses will attend. No special section will predominate, Mr. Serkin said, and he added that a remarkably broad balance of instruments will result from the representation.

The Brattleboro Daily Reformer, 1951

Adolf Busch, Rudolf Serkin, Herman Busch.

Marlboro's founders—Marcel Moyse, Louis Moyse, Rudolf Serkin, Blanche Moyse, Adolf Busch, Herman Busch (with cellist Nathan Chaikin second from left).

A Dedication to Art

The music at Marlboro turned out to be more exciting than the rolling foothills of the Green Mountains, and heaven knows they have a matchless rhythm blending softness and ruggedness. For here was not just a little festival designed as an innocent summer amusement or as bait for tourists. Here was music-making in its finest and most joyous state. Here was a dedication to art that could be an inspiration for months to come.

There is nothing pretentious about Marlboro. The site is a remote hillside about midway between Bennington and Brattleboro. The buildings and grounds are those of the campus of Marlboro College, a modest institution that provides for some thirty students during the academic year. There are only a few white clapboard buildings, which look as if they were once part of a farm.

. . . It happened that some distinguished musicians— the late Adolf Busch, the violinist; his son-in-law, Mr. Serkin, and Marcel Moyse, the flutist, and his musical family—had decided to take up residence in this area of New England. They were approached and invited to do something musically.

Concerts were held in the dining hall until 1962.

Not Another Series of Concerts

These musicians were not interested in setting up another series of concerts. But they were eager to make a contribution. They felt that there were possibilities to be explored in ensemble music. They were especially convinced that professional performers, busy with their normal duties during the winter, did not have time enough to immerse themselves in chamber music.

As Mr. Serkin remarked the other day, orchestral players need a change from the discipline of conductors and their batons. Some conductors, he added, had recommended musicians from their own ensembles who would benefit from a chance to express themselves and to learn something of the rewards of spontaneity.

The Marlboro Family–1951.

(Top) Blanche Moyse, Rudolf Serkin. *(Bottom)* Max Rabinovitsj, two unidentified artists, Felix Galimir, Yuan Tung.

(Top) Bernard Goldberg, Louis Moyse, Luis Batlle. *(Bottom)* Alexander Schneider in rehearsal in the dining hall.

The Spirit of Chamber Music

The object of the summer season remains what it was at the outset—to cultivate the spirit of chamber music, which is like a democracy of art. Each musician is encouraged to explore a wide repertory and, more important, his own feelings and resources.

"This kind of thing could happen only in America," Mr. Serkin said later. Somehow it belongs in Vermont, and one hopes it can stay there, finding the financial support it richly deserves. It should not become bigger. Its raison d'être is what it does for musicians.

. . . On this Vermont hilltop commercialism seems not to exist, and should never intrude.

Howard Taubman,
The New York Times, 1956

James Levine, Van Cliburn.

(Top) Ernestine Briesmeister Schor, Claude Frank, Alicia Schachter, Isaac Stern. *(Bottom)* Harold Wright, Benita Valente, Rudolf Serkin.

(Top) Lawrence Chelsi, Herbert Coursey, Martial Singher. *(Bottom)* Myron Bloom, Rudolf Serkin.

A Family Affair

"Marlboro is a community of artists, something like an Israeli kibbutz or perhaps like a Soviet commune as they would like it to be," Mr. Serkin told a festival visitor. "Nowhere else will you find this complete lack of selfishness, this coming together of musicians from all countries and all backgrounds, this dedication to the composer and his music rather than to the performer's glory."

In all his life, Mr. Serkin went on, he has encountered only one other place where such a spirit prevailed. "That was in the home of a Mrs. Schwartzwald in Vienna when I was a small boy." That home, he said, was a gathering spot for the significant artists of the time, a time that brought the young Bohemian pianist into contact with such catalytic artists as Oskar Kokoschka, the painter; Rainer Maria Rilke, the poet; and Arnold Schoenberg, the 12-tone composer with whom Mr. Serkin studied composition.

The Marlboro Festival, which takes place each summer on the campus of Marlboro College in the Green Mountains, actually began "as a family affair," Mr. Serkin said. He and his father-in-law, Adolf Busch, the violinist, started a summer music program on the campus along with Adolf's brother, Herman Busch, the cellist, and their close friends Marcel, Louis and Blanche Moyse. "Before long," Mr. Serkin said, "we found that the students coming to the festival were as good as the faculty. So we began calling everyone a participant."

The emphasis that Mr. Serkin insists upon, said Frank Salomon, the co-administrator of the festival, works so well that musicians in other countries are beginning to refer to "Marlboro sessions"—sessions, that is, in which senior musicians play "not as coaches but as equals within the group." There are no students and no teachers.

Donal Henahan, *The New York Times,* 1975

Zvi Zeitlin, Claude Frank, unidentified, Stephen Manes, Michael Rudiakov, Caroline Woron Levine.

(Top) Jaime Laredo, Alexander Schneider. *(Bottom)* Unidentified, Arnold Steinhardt, Marcel Moyse, Ruth Wright.

THE FOUNDING, THE EARLY YEARS, THE CONCEPT

A *Serkin Fantasia on a Theme by Busch*

This concept that music has meaningfulness apart from public performances to vast audiences permeates the Marlboro studios and rehearsal halls in a way that sets the place apart from any summer music activity I have encountered. Other summer music schools aim everything at the performances for paying customers. This one aims at the improvement of the musicians, and the audiences that get a chance to look in on this rehabilitory rite go away edified. Music-making did not start at Marlboro quite the way it ended up. "We began here ten years ago giving faculty concerts," Serkin said, "but then the students became so good that they took over." Since then the dividing line between the Marlboro teaching staff and its student body has been a diffuse one, and there were moments in my talks with Serkin when I had the fleeting impression that the pianist most other pianists regard as "the master" regarded himself as the school's sole student and the other ninety musicians on the premises as his teachers. The locale perhaps induces that receptive stance in him, for Serkin regarded Adolf Busch, the violinist who

lived in nearby Guilford and who died eight years ago, with the same tutorial reverence as dozens of superb young American musicians regard Serkin. When he first met Busch in Vienna in 1920 Serkin was seventeen. The pair played Beethoven sonatas together in European recitals, and fled together from Germany in 1933 to settle in Switzerland, where Serkin married Busch's daughter Irene in 1935. In the late Thirties the Busch–Serkin troupe settled in the U.S. and ultimately in the Vermont hills around Marlboro. In addition to its principals there were Busch's cello–playing brother Herman, the flutist Marcel Moyse with his son Louis and Blanche Moyse and a steady succession of beleaguered European emigres who depended on the Buschs to provide political asylum, square meals and chamber music. It was in this setting that the pianist first savored the pleasures of a community of musicians, and in a very real sense the Marlboro school is the result—a Serkin fantasia on a theme by Adolf Busch.

Joseph Roddy, *Vermont Life,* 1960

(Top) Alexander Schneider, Herman Busch, Rudolf Serkin. *(Bottom)* Arnold Steinhardt, Philipp Naegele, Jules Eskin, Michael Tree.

(Top) Ornulf Gulbransen, John Mack, Louise Scribner, John Van Bockern. *(Bottom)* Jaime Laredo, John Dalley, Jules Eskin, Endel Kalam, Harry Zaratzian.

Concerts in a Converted Cow Barn

The most exciting chamber music recitals in the U.S. originate in a wooden box in a small, white clapboard cottage in Vermont. Into the box go requests for performances of everything from Mozart to Schoenberg; out of the box come twice-weekly concerts played in a converted cow barn by some of the world's most famed and gifted instrumentalists. Last week the barn echoed to Beethoven's *Sextet in E-Flat*, Martinu's *Three Madrigals for Violin and Viola* and Bach's *Brandenberg Concerto No. 5*. Occasion: a concert at Vermont's Marlboro Festival, now celebrating its tenth season.

Fortunato Arico, Philipp Naegele, Marc Gottlieb.

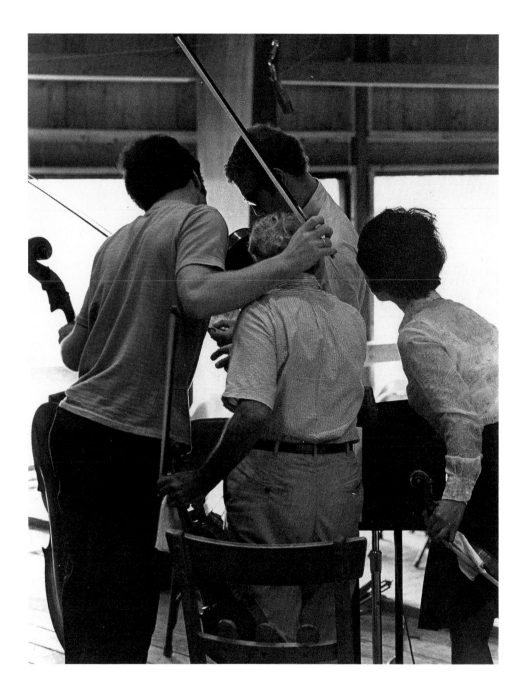

Concerts Never Planned More Than
a Day or Two in Advance

... For his "Republic of Equals," Serkin decided to have no faculty in the normal sense ("We are all students") and no formal course of instruction. Instead, the 90–odd instrumentalists who attend Marlboro every summer pay $500 apiece for their six–week stay, split up into informal quartets, quintets, or chamber orches- tras, depending on what music they want to play. The public concerts are never planned more than a day or two in advance, and consist of pieces the resident musi- cians have chosen by putting their nominations in the suggestion box.

Time Magazine, 1960

Ronald Leonard, Scott Nickrenz, Felix Galimir, Yoko Matsuda. FACING PAGE: Richard Mackey.

THE MUSIC, THE PEOPLE

The Persons Auditorium, built in 1962.

A Republic of Equals

Outside the dining hall on the campus of Marlboro College, summer home of the Marlboro Music School, hangs a large board. The hours of the day run down a column on the left; across the top are listed eleven possible locations ... Cards affixed to the board list the chamber works being prepared hour by hour in each of these locations, and the board is usually completely filled.

The job of filling the board belongs to Endel Kalam, a violist from Boston who is also one of the performers at the school. Mr. Kalam must make the complex matching of available performers to available repertory, and allocate the proper personnel for the performance of the fifty chamber works for all conceivable combinations that may be performed at Marlboro on any given day. Mr. Kalam's job is complicated the more because most of the ninety participants at the school have requested in advance particular works they would like to play.

It is the peculiar nature of Marlboro's approach to music that creates Mr. Kalam's problems. Ordinarily, one thinks of a music school as a place where a given group of faculty members decides on a repertory, and assigns it to students who have no recourse.

Alexander Schneider and chamber orchestra perform Vivaldi in the new hall. FACING PAGE *(Top)* Jaime Laredo, Arnold Steinhardt, Michael Tree. *(Bottom)* The scheduling board.

But Marlboro has no faculty, it is only a "school" for want of a more accurate title, and thinks of its members rather as "participants" than "students."

... explained Rudolf Serkin, president of the school and one of its founders, "over the years it became clear that the main thing that was happening here was that people were getting together to make music. Those of us who first thought of ourselves as 'teachers' found that we were learning as many things as the 'students' were. And so, gradually we became that ideal sort of thing, a 'republic of equals.'"

Alan Rich, *The New York Times,* 1962

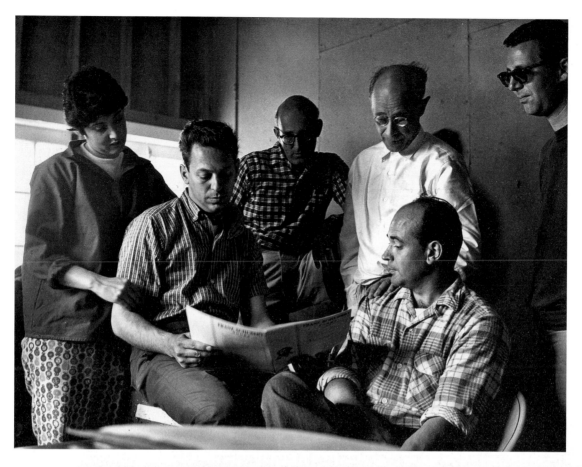

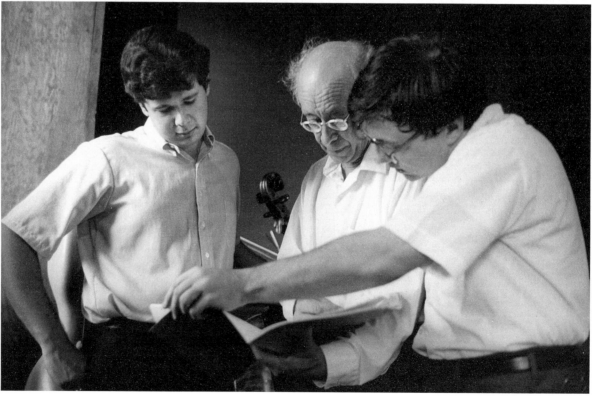

(Top) A playback session with Benita Valente, Anthony Checchia, record producer Howard Scott, Rudolf Serkin, Harold Wright, and Paul Boyer. *(Bottom)* Robert Sylvester, Rudolf Serkin, unidentified.

Unlimited Rehearsal Time

Talent alone, of course, is not enough. What the brilliant young professionals get up here are direction and rehearsal. Lots of rehearsal. No music is put on the weekend programs unless it is completely prepared. The Schoenberg "Kammersymphonie," a difficult work for 15 solo instruments, had the benefit of some 20 rehearsals under the direction of Rudolf Kolisch, Schoenberg's son–in–law, who led from the first violin desk. In New York a performance might get three rehearsals—maybe."

Harold C. Schonberg,
The New York Times, 1964

(Top) Felix Galimir, Donald Weilerstein, Fortunato Arico, Philipp Naegele, Nobuko Imai, and Joyce Kelley (at table). *(Bottom)* Boris Kroyt.

Harry Sargous, Blanche Moyse, Stephanie Przybylska.

(Top left) Mieczyslaw Horszowski, Paula Robison. *(Top right)* Sol Schoenbach, Mordecai Rechtman. *(Bottom)* Kendall Betts, John Swallow, Edmond Moore, Henry Nowak, Wilmer Wise.

Music of Their Own Choosing

... The idea was to establish a setting where musicians—the best musicians, young and old—could congregate, discourse, and play music altogether of their own choosing, working on it in interchange until their understanding and mastery of it satisfied even themselves. Any concertizing would be strictly incidental. This still goes. The pianist Leon Fleisher said last summer: "After all, a human being's greatest joy is sharing experiences with others in an endeavor. And undeniably some of the greatest music ever written, the most nearly divine, if you don't mind the word, is chamber music."

John M. Conly, *The Reporter,* 1964

Philipp Naegele, Heiichiro Ohyama, Rudolf Serkin.

(Top) Alexander Schneider, Pina Carmirelli, Felix Galimir. *(Bottom)* Mieczyslaw Horszowski, Felix Galimir.

(Top) Samuel Rhodes, Hiroko Yajima. (Bottom) Nobuko Imai, Isidore Cohen.

Music for the Joy of it

... Marlboro is basically a mystique, and the mystique involves a special spirit of relaxation—the playing of music in salonlike surroundings just for the joy of it, and not for the sake of climbing some particular peak of accomplishment in the furiously competitive world often referred to among professionals (in some ways quite appropriately) as "the music racket".

... The experience was so entirely pleasant that I had an uneasy feeling that as a critic I was out of place; the performances were not being given in order to be judged but in order to bring about a rare kind of musical enjoyment.

The New Yorker, 1966

Elaine Lee, Isidore Cohen, Louis Opalesky, Wilmer Wise, Henry Nowak.

(Top) Eve Dickens, Marcel Moyse. *(Bottom)* Marcel Moyse and a woodwind octet.

Marcel Moyse.

Listen to What the Composer
is Trying to Say

To define the genius of Marcel Moyse, the celebrated flutist who was one of the founders of the Marlboro Music School and Festival, and still presides there over the studies of the more advanced woodwind professional, it would seem easiest to quote the old adage—"an infinite capacity for taking pains." One has only to attend one of his master classes, or listen to him directing an instrumental ensemble, or for that matter, to talk informally with him in rare moments of leisure, to realize how apt this is in his case.

"Color, more bright color, like that painting of my native countryside on the wall over there," he implores his students. "Do not play the notes only, please, listen in your hearts to what the composer is trying to say, and help him a little." With a quizzical little smile he continues, "Do not mistake me, do not go off into wild emotional flights of individual fancy. Stick to the original pattern but color it with loving care, for otherwise you are in danger of producing monotony which is a very bad thing in chamber music."

. . . "I don't want you to misunderstand me about the matter of emotional coloring in musical interpretation. I have no use in my classes or elsewhere, for the actor who plays to the gallery, like the fiddler in an Hungarian restaurant. A musician must feel deeply, but to make others understand what his instrument is saying, he must be natural, honest, and sincere, and forget himself."

Mary M. Cushing,
The Brattleboro Daily Reformer, 1960

Marcel Moyse. FACING PAGE *(Top)* Mischa Schneider, Harry Zaratzian. *(Bottom)* Blanche Moyse and the Brattleboro Music Center Chorus and Orchestra in the annual Bach concert, hosted by Marlboro Music.

The Playing's the Thing

. . . the fact that Marlboro "wasn't planned, it just grew," as Serkin says, seems to contribute to the authenticity of what goes on there.

Of 80 Works, Only 5 or 6 Will be Chosen

Marlboro may be the only music festival in existence to which musicians, who pay for the privilege, are invited with the specific warning (and this in writing) not to attend with the expectation of giving public performances. This is the key to its special quality: the playing's the thing; it goes on quite literally all day, six and a half days a week, in the nine college buildings available for the purpose. Out of perhaps eighty chamber works in progress during any week, five or six will be chosen for the Saturday and Sunday concerts open to the public. . .

Shirley Fleming, *High Fidelity*, 1966

(Right) Steven Jackson, Joaquin Valdepeñas.

Pablo Casals, Marta Casals, Rudolf Serkin.

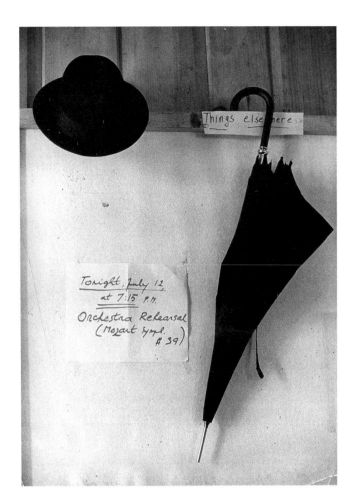

All are Here to Learn

Pablo Casals, who spent the last summers of his life at Marlboro, until his death in 1973 at the age of 96, spoke of the uniqueness of this approach when he said, "I don't know anything equal to it. I know many musical centers for every country—Russia, Germany, London and so on. But like Marlboro, nothing. Here, all those people come and all of them with great talent—they will become celebrities, many of them. But all of them are here to learn. All of them. You don't find that in any other place. And this is why I love to come here."

Gretchen Becker, *Vermont Summer,*
Supplement to *The Bennington Banner*
and the *Brattleboro Reformer,* 1980

(Bottom) Pablo Casals, Patricia Parr, Michael Grebanier.

1960 was the first of Pablo Casals' thirteen summers at Marlboro.

An Arcady of Music

Over the years, I have held classes in many parts of the world—in Paris, Berlin, Zermatt, Tokyo and other places—but the mood in Marlboro is unique. The surroundings themselves . . . hold for me an ineffable charm and loveliness. I know of no place where I am more conscious of the affinity between nature and music. Marlboro is a veritable Arcady of music! And the approach to music too has a special quality.

Pablo Casals, Special guest,
1960, 1962–1973

Pablo Casals, Camilla Doppmann.

The Blend of Young Fire with Searching Musicianship

I had heard of Marlboro, of course, and from recordings I knew its standards were high. But, like most visitors from the other side of the Atlantic, I was pretty vague about what actually went on there. I envisaged a rather choice festival in rural surroundings. But when I learned that programs were only announced 48 hours in advance my heart sank. Was this another of those little gatherings of the select, dedicated to putting the outsider in his place?

... In fact, my first evening there brought one of the most enthralling concerts I havè had the good fortune to attend. ... what held me spellbound was the blend of young fire with searching musicianship, which I have subsequently come to recognize as characteristically Marlborian. Every detail was vividly articulated yet experienced in the context of the music's development.

But this was only a curtain–raiser. for what was to come. ... I have heard performances of Beethoven's Seventh Symphony in all shapes and sizes, but I swear I have never experienced the equal of what Casals unleashed on that torrid Saturday evening in a small barn tucked away in the woods and hills of Vermont.

The very sound—80 first-rate instrumentalists playing as though their lives depended on it is in itself something you don't often hear in a concert hall—had an open, unblended, almost rough quality that seemed to me essentially Beethovenian. From the first of those momentous rising scales in the introduction to the first movement, sheer musical impulse was overwhelming: Trenchant rhythms, a bold and sweeping sense of line and a compelling grasp of musical argument all generated an almost implacable sense of purpose. And when first the oboes and then the strings sang out their calming answer to this elemental fury, it was as if the very essence of Beethoven's heroic humanity were incarnate in sound. How can I communicate the rough–hewn directness of that sublime performance? It was, as another member of the audience later said, "a roaring lion."

Unlike so many other festivals that achieve high standards, the programs at Marlboro preserve a life-enhancing freshness. There is scarcely a concert that does not bring a new experience.

But, as American readers don't need to be told by

a visiting critic, concerts are a mere by–product of Marlboro's activities. Its real purpose is to provide a retreat for artists from the grueling treadmill of concert life. It is a place where mature musicians can recover their wind and deepen their art in companionship with others just on the brink of their careers.

Marlboro's refusal to allow itself to be yoked to a concert schedule seems to me abundantly justified. To announce programs in advance would be to set up just those pressures that are an inescapable part of a musician's life in the 20th century. And year by year they grow more remorseless. From processed food we are well on the way to processed music—and I am not referring to gramophone records. The jet has revolutionized concert life. It has created a world in which top–ranking artists spend much of a year circling the globe, each with his special act. As a result, more people have access to more first–rate performances than ever before. But at what a price!

The standardization of repertory and performers, growing so that what you hear in Tokyo and Amsterdam is much the same as in Vienna and Chicago, is bad enough. But the effect on the artists themselves is likely to prove worse. What can be the state of mind of a pianist for whom the future is a vista of hotel rooms and an unending series of performances of Beethoven's *G major Piano Concerto*?

In the final resort, musical life depends on the musician's responsiveness to what he performs, and how can this hope to survive. . . ? Indeed, there are already signs enough of the damage that they are causing among young musicians who so heedlessly embrace the perpetuum mobile of the international merry–go–round.

In conditions such as these it is no wonder that musicians who can command substantial fees prefer to set their summers aside for refreshment at Marlboro, where they are not paid a penny, even if they perform in public. Far from being a precious cult, Marlboro has become a dire necessity, an oasis in a desert of commercialized, stereotyped music-making. It is a life–giving spring of just those energies that the remainder of musical life is consuming so recklessly.

Peter Heyworth, *The New York Times,* 1969

Pablo Casals, Mrs. and Mr. Zoltan Kodaly.

Who Plays with Whom?

Things are run on a nicely anarchistic basis. . . . The logistics involve the musical dispersal of some 80 thoroughbred virtuosos on all instruments. Who plays with whom? What kind of repertory do they tackle? How are they getting along? Are there personality problems? Technical mismatches? Most participants have about 20 to 35 weekly hours of work. During the summer a clarinet player might run through music by Françaix, Hindemith, Mozart, Brahms, Reicha, Beethoven, Martinu, Naginski, Nováček, Strauss, Janáček, Prokofiev, Goossens and Bach. (This was the actual repertory of a player's schedule not long ago.)

Julius Levine, Barbara Wilson, Samuel Rhodes.

Those Who Come to the Concerts
Take Potluck

Anarchy comes in when the weekly festival programs
are to be arranged. Often they are not made up until
the night before the concert. With all of the talent
around, there is much more music to choose from than
could possibly be played. The more experienced "faculty" members decide on those performances best prepared by the musicians. Those who come to the concerts necessarily take potluck. They may get Bach, they
may get Berg, and there is no way of knowing. As yet
there have been no complaints.

Harold C. Schonberg,
The New York Times, 1964

(Top) Sol Schoenbach and a woodwind serenade. *(Bottom)* The new week's schedule board about to be posted.

(Top) Christopher Lantz' *Entreaty* for soprano, violin, cello, flute, piano and timpani, led by the composer. *(Bottom)* Luigi Dallapiccola.

Not Limited to Standard Repertoire

The musical interests of Marlboro are by no means limited to standard repertoire. Resident composers last summer, who worked at length with players on performances of their own music, were Leon Kirchner, David Del Tredici, and Tison Street. In the expansive spirit of these surroundings they are able to take their time in a manner which would be impossible in the hard commercial drive of big–city concertizing, when every hour of rehearsals cuts deep into somebody's bank account. Kirchner's *Concerto for Violin, Cello, Ten Solo Winds, and Percussion,* for example, got fifteen hours of rehearsal before its 1965 performance at Marlboro—an allotment of time all but impossible under normal working conditions.

Shirley Fleming, *High Fidelity,* 1966

Henry Weinberg's *Movement for String Quartet* with Paul Katz, Nobuko Imai, the composer, Felix Galimir, and Endre Granat.

Leon Kirchner, who played a major role in the study and performance of new music at Marlboro.

Rehearsing Rather Than Performing

What happens in this lofty Vermont hideaway is a cease-less routine of rehearsing rather than performing, for this is a festival for musicians rather than the music–lovers. Above all, it is a renewal and re–inspiration for great artists who modern life lurches from too little sleep to train or airport, to recording studio, to rehearsal, to concert, to hotel.

Each artist learns as he plays (and he plays again and again). One can, indeed, hardly exaggerate the insight to be gained amid constantly changing groups of players of the highest calibre and from rehearsing in depth.

(Top) Karen Dreyfus, Felix Galimir, Julius Levine, Colin Carr. *(Bottom)* Lisa Lancaster, Mischa Schneider.

A Variety of Musical Experience

Records are kept (this is a nightmare for the organizers) of how many hours A plays with each of B to Z. If A is foolish enough to show signs of settling pleasurably with one colleague or another, he gets promptly moved on, for the idea at Marlboro is to impart a variety of musical experience and keep musicians on the move.

(Top) Yuzuko Horigome, David Soyer. *(Bottom left)* Yuzuko Horigome, Mei-Chen Liao. *(Bottom right)* Hiroko Yajima, Andras Schiff.

Paul Tortelier, Wilhelmina Smith.

(Top) John Nesbit, Luis Batlle, Donald Collup, Daniel Pincus. *(Bottom)* Yo Yo Ma, Sandor Vegh.

(Top) A rehearsal of Beethoven's *Choral Fantasy. (Bottom left)* Julie Landsman, Claude Frank. (Bottom right) Luis Batlle, Gregory Hopkins.

Teaching Sensitivity

Working with non–kindred spirits in chamber music is deemed to be as educating as blending with the like–minded; it teaches sensitivity, balance and the art of accommodating, not to mention diplomacy. "You have to be very tactful, after a rehearsal," one cellist told me. "If you announce 'your tone was hard, steely and loud and destroyed everything sensitive I was trying to do,' it may be quite true but it is not the way to improve response at the next session."

Daisy Newman, Donald Hermanns.

(Top) Bart Feller, Luis Batlle, Carl Halvorson, Michael Matthews. *(Bottom)* Mischa Schneider, Ida Levin, Carmit Zori.

(Top) Felix Galimir, Erika Nickrenz, Marina Piccinini, Todd Palmer, Christopher Costanza. *(Bottom)* Peter Wiley, Catherine Metz, Takumi Kubota.

(Top) Paula Robison, Felix Galimir, Richard Stoltzman, Murray Perahia, Ronald Leonard. *(Bottom)* Georgine Resick, Carl Halvorson, Mary Westbrook-Geha.

Marlboro is Where You Come to Learn Second Violin

Serkin puts it more tersely: "Marlboro demands a spirit of generosity." (That applies not least to the allocation of parts—"Marlboro is where you come to learn second violin," Serkin adds). Generosity, happily, is widely evident—and any outstanding scores can be settled in the Marlboro ritual of hurling screwed up napkin balls after lunch or dinner.

Godfrey Barker, *The Daily Telegraph,* 1986

(Top) Mieczyslaw Horszowski, Yuuko Shiokawa. *(Bottom)* Eugene Drucker, Felix Galimir. FACING PAGE *(Top)* Mitsuko Uchida. (Bottom) Thomas Lorango, Bruno Canino.

THE MUSIC, THE PEOPLE 59

Everyone is a Student Here

"Everyone is a student here," its director, the great pianist Rudolf Serkin, once told an interviewer. When his listener looked skeptical, Serkin insisted it was true.

"There's always something to learn. When I hear a wind player or a singer phrase, it's different from what I am hearing the rest of the year playing by myself. And there is always some work that all of us are hearing for the first time."

Walking around the campus on a cloudy Saturday afternoon, you can hear music coming from almost every building.

In a former blacksmith's shop, a piano quintet is playing; a dozen people sit or stand outside the door listening. The dining hall has that food smell common to dining halls, but the music for flute and strings being rehearsed is like no dining hall music I ever heard.

Saturday night, in the handsome concert hall, the music making is of a very special order. The pieces are rare, the performing spectacularly good.

That seems to be the spirit of Marlboro. You can feel it, even in a short weekend. It is still something of a family affair—the brilliant Yan Pascal Tortelier is Paul's son; Judith Serkin, who played fine cello in a Mozart trio Sunday, is one of Rudolf Serkin's six children—but in a larger sense, Marlboro seems a true family of musicians—that very community which Adolf Busch dreamed of so long ago.

William C. Glacklin, *The Sacramento Bee,* 1977

Joel Krosnick, Steven Tenenbom.

Isidore Cohen, Ralph De Souza, Peter Lloyd, Astrid Schween, Benjamin Simon.

He Changed Our Lives

He spoke to us with a rare honesty and commitment, not through his words but through his music and example—

In a time when society seemed to value success above all else, he demanded far more from us and from himself.

At Marlboro, he created a true and lasting family, not just an institution. He made us all strive to be better than we were. He changed our lives.

We celebrate the life of Rudolf Serkin and all he gave us. We pledge to maintain Marlboro and its ideals and thereby honor his memory.

> The Musicians, Trustees, Officers, Staff
> and Friends of Marlboro Music
> *The New York Times,*
> May 19, 1991

Rudolf Serkin, Harold Wright.

(Top) Rudolf Serkin, Herman Busch. *(Bottom)* Rudolf Serkin, Leslie Parnas, Jaime Laredo.

(Top) Cecile Licad, David Soyer, Rudolf Serkin. *(Bottom)* Rudolf Serkin, Sharon Robinson.

Beethoven's Choral Fantasy

Some old grads travel back each summer to size up their successors and hear them perform what amounts to the school song—Beethoven's Choral Fantasy for orchestra, chorus, and piano with Serkin as the pianist, the last work played at the Festival each year. The chorus jamming the stage includes just about all at Marlboro who are not in the orchestra: clerical staff, a visiting trustee or two, and a clutch of local residents.

Last season during the Choral Fantasy, just before its exhilarating finale, all on stage saw Serkin plain: Begin-ners resist doing it and professionals deride those who do, but there was the great man counting time with pursed lips, holding a difficult trill for its full six beats, in a work he had performed over a hundred times. The sight of their old idol still so unvain in his art, followed by the choral fanfaronade of "Music's flood our life sur-rounds" set off unashamed tears on stage and some out front.

Joseph Roddy, *Yankee,* 1985

Alexander Schneider, Rudolf Serkin.

Beethoven's *Choral Fantasy*

(Top) Yuzuko Horigome, Rudolf Serkin. *(Bottom)* Rudolf Serkin, Felix Galimir.

Mischa Schneider, unidentified child, Jerry Grossman, Rudolf Serkin, Frank Salomon, Pamela Frame.

... I said the festival was unique, and so it is. It denies, first of all, that it even *is* a festival; every player invited gets a letter containing the extraordinary injunction: 'No one should attend with the intention of performing.' And what that means rapidly becomes clear.

For the participants at Marlboro come here not to play in concerts, but simply to work together on the chamber music repertoire. ... In the week I stayed, there were 63 items in rehearsal; they included six by Beethoven, seven by Mozart, three by Schubert, four by Schumann, three by Brahms, two by Haydn, three by Dvořák, two by Mendelssohn and two, one of them included *in memoriam*, by the American composer Samuel Barber, who died earlier this year. The rest included works by Max Bruch, Boccherini, Debussy, Arnold Bax, Edmund Rubbra, Ravel, Dittersdorf, Dohnányi, César Franck, Hindemith ... Mahler, Purcell, Max Reger, Schoenberg, Weber, Sibelius, Prokofiev and Joachim Raff.

From this vast and eclectic repertoire, the items to be publicly performed, almost as an afterthought, are chosen; and the concert programmes are never announced more than a day or two in advance—not from caprice, but because they are not decided before then. And in the method of their selection lies another proof that Marlboro is unique, and this perhaps the most important proof of all. The great majority of the participants are young; many are still at musical colleges or academies, some just at the outset of professional careers, a few more established. And amid this gathering of burgeoning talent, chosen by audition from among the cream of the world's musical young people, there is a seasoning of veterans, who play with the youngsters not as teachers with pupils, but as searchers after musical truth, in which search all, young and old, are equals: in a quartet or quintet or other work with two violins or two cellos, it is the experienced player who takes the second part, and the beginner who is the leader. And as the preparation goes on, a consensus gradually emerges as to which items are best fitted to form part of the programme of the concerts that conclude the week.

Nobody dictates, nobody decrees, nobody insists. And that, incidentally, is just as true at the other end of the Marlboro process. When I inquired how the works to be studied are chosen, I was amazed to learn that all the participants are asked, when they get their invitations, to nominate the music they wish to work on; there follows the construction of a vast jigsaw puzzle, designed to ensure that every player, as far as is humanly possible, is accommodated in the music of his or her choice.

... it is Serkin's noble spirit that pervades this enchanted place. He is clearly adored by the young participants, though they stand in no awe of him, and indeed are not above suddenly pelting him with bread rolls in the dining hall, where there are no hierarchies and no tables reserved for the seniors, and where everyone takes it in turn to clean up afterwards. This place is indeed a true fraternity, the members united in their love of music and their desire to serve the greatest of the arts, and Rudolf Serkin, with half a century of achievement behind him, is as much music's servant as the most wide–eyed 18-year-old.

Perhaps that makes Marlboro sound solemn, which would be the most inappropriate word imaginable. It's really like a huge, boisterous family—indeed, many of the participants come *en famille*, and the dining hall resounds to the noise of children ...

... Most rehearsal periods are of two hours, and it was fascinating to hear a work gradually taking shape through the week, the players getting closer and closer to the heart of the music. The young musicians rapidly develop a remarkable interchange of criticism, comment and mutual encouragement; no one defers to the veterans merely because they *are* veterans, and such widely experienced players as the violinist Felix Galimir, the cellist David Soyer and the double–bass player Julius Levine were always as ready to listen as to speak.

There is a Marlboro atmosphere, a Marlboro spirit; is there a Marlboro style? They deny it, but not very vehemently, and the sweetness of tone and richness of feeling that I heard being striven for in work after work do, I think, add up to a consistent approach. In the Mozart quintet, the favourite word of David Soyer, the cellist, who could give at least 25 years to any of the other players, was '*espressivo*', and if I had suggested that they might hang over the entrance to Marlboro a banner with '*espressivo*' written on it, nobody would have been surprised. Loving expressiveness sums up the music made at this place, and it is surely no accident that Rudolf Serkin has for so many years been supreme in the great Viennese classics where expressiveness is all.

Bernard Levin, *The Listener,* 1981

Constantly Refining, Searching, Questioning

It is this intensity of music–making which makes Marlboro so very special and so different from most other festivals. We were constantly refining, searching, questioning, and striving to uphold the highest possible standards. Each player, regardless of age, experience, or even professional stature, was totally involved in the music. A young, aspiring musician might have felt intimidated while working with such renowned chamber music "veterans" as Felix Galimir, Isidore Cohen, Julius Levine, Pina Carmirelli, and Sol Schoen-bach (who was Director of the Settlement Music School in Philadelphia for some twenty-five years and a regular Marlboro participant from 1967 to 1982). But in this musical "republic of equals" there was a give–and–take within each group that resulted in concentrated performances of great intensity. Only the music mattered—and whether it was played with integrity and conviction.

Lydia Artymiw,
Marlboro Participant, 1972–74

Rudolf Serkin.

(Top) Unidentified, Margaret Batjer. *(Bottom)* Young Uck Kim, Felix Galimir.

(Top) Caroline Levine, Hatto Beyerle. *(Bottom)* Sara Sant'Ambrogio, Matthias Naegele, Ida Levin.

Learning From One Another

Unique is the only word for the place.

At any time of the day or early evening, one hears music coming from everywhere. From 9 to 6, the Marlboro community is rehearsing...

Unlike most music camps or summer festivals involving students, Marlboro is designed so the professional musician—or student with professional experience—can work with other professionals, refining chamber pieces of their own choosing.

There is no student–teacher relationship per se. Rather, young professionals can work with a Rudolf Serkin, a Felix Galimir, Pina Carmirelli, or Julius Levine, sharing ideas, learning from one another, finding the way to make a piece work for the group assembled.

(Top) Frederick Moyer, Sara Sant'Ambrogio, Bruno Giuranna. *(Bottom)* Rudolph Vrbsky, Scott Janusch, Alexander Heller.

Returning to Share Their Knowledge

There are, in fact, three "age groups" at Marlboro—not necessarily related to the age of their members: the young newcomers, who come back for as many as four seasons . . .; the "middle-aged," who have been Marlboro participants in the past and are now returning to share their knowledge and eventually become members of the "senior" musicians, such as Serkin, Galimir, and Marcel Moyse, who are the artistic motivating force behind the institution.

(Top) Rudolph Vrbsky. *(Bottom)* Robert Routch, John Serkin. FACING PAGE Laurie Smukler, Carol Wincenc.

(Top) Ida Levin, Carmit Zori. *(Bottom)* Pina Carmirelli, Lucy Stoltzman.

Sandor Vegh and chamber orchestra.

A Group Effort

Though there is one senior member in each rehearsing ensemble, it is a group effort, and often—because of the intensity of the rehearsal schedule—first-chair orchestral musicians and even major soloists come to the festival so they can work on a few pieces they have never had the time to polish fully in the course of their normal activities. . . . Mr. Checchia, Salomon, and Serkin share the view that it will remain a tradition passed on from young to old as they become a part of the Marlboro family.

(Top) Suzanne Handel, David Starobin, Michael Parloff, Karen Smith. *(Bottom)* Elaine Douvas, John Ferrillo. FACING PAGE *(Top)* Carolyn Davis, David Jolley, Stefanie Przybylska, Joaquin Valdepeñas, Gunther Schuller. *(Middle)* David Soyer, Yuzuko Horigome, Marian Hahn. *(Bottom)* Ida Levin, Tomoko Kato, Siegfried Palm, Gail Kruvand.

The Spirit of Generosity

Mr. Salomon refers to the spirit of generosity that pervades all aspects of the operation. It is something a visitor can sense if he stays for more than one day, and it is manifested in the artists' generosity toward their colleagues (as well as the less visible non-artists' generosity toward the institution).

Mr. Galimir notes that "there is no other place like it—the enthusiasm, the dedication, you don't find it anywhere else. People enjoy what they're doing, and they enjoy each other."

Thor Eckert, Jr.,
The Christian Science Monitor, 1980

(Left) Timothy Cobb, Michelle Reed. *(Right)* Young Uck Kim, Judith Mendenhall, Jennie Hansen.

(Top) Clelia Goldings, Cynthia Raim, Chris Komer. *(Bottom)* Hiroko Yajima, Ronald Leonard, Lee Luvisi, Jennie Hansen, John Graham, Julius Levine.

THE MUSIC, THE PEOPLE

Learning to Serve Music

Well, Marlboro for me—as I am sure for everyone who ever attended it—was a turning point. It had a crucial effect on my repertoire as well as on my whole approach to music. This can be summed up in the advice I now always give my students: "It is not only solitary practice that will make you grow. It is learning to serve music in every area and with all humility."

Zvi Zeitlin,
Marlboro Participant, 1959–61, 1963

(Left) Claude Frank, Matt Haimovitz. *(Right)* Lilian Kallir, Sara Sant'Ambrogio, Katherine Murdock.

The Process of Understanding

... There was always at Marlboro the sense that the essence of preparing a piece was the process of understanding the music, of truly "interpreting." Music is an abstract language, and only the phonetic pronunciation is put down on the page along with a few written clues; one must allow oneself to intuitively sense the meaning of the phrases and the turns and twists of the plot. The best way of learning a language is to live with people who speak that language, and for learning the language of music Marlboro is the ideal environment.

Lucy Stoltzman, Marlboro Participant,
1973–76, 1981, 1990

Ron Chen-Zion, Carol Wincenc, Asako Urushihara, Hillel Zori, Bruno Canino.

Where I Began Questioning Things in Music

Marlboro was the place where I decided to become a musician and, more importantly, where I met my future wife.

The four summers I spent at Marlboro were great formative years. It was there that I was first exposed to the fellowship of colleagues young and old. It was there that legendary names became real human beings. And it was there that I began questioning things in music.

Living through these summers, experiencing the great chamber music literature for the first time, led me to a commitment to music that I could not have received from one school or one teacher. I believe that the sense of fun, camaraderie, and common culture found at Marlboro remain with me as the essential elements of good music making and the dedication of the fathers of the festival. . .

Yo-Yo Ma, Marlboro Participant, 1972–73, 1975–76

(Top) Kai Vogler, Roglit Ishay, Siegfried Palm. *(Bottom)* Marie-Luise Neunecker, Rudolph Vrbsky.

Joshua Bell, Asako Urushihara, Richard Goode.

THE MUSIC, THE PEOPLE

Musical Standards

Because I did not attend a conservatory, and because I came to a decision to pursue a musical career comparatively late in my life, Marlboro played an especially critical role in my development—perhaps even more so than for hundreds of other professional musicians who count Marlboro among their most important influences. I performed in concerts with Pablo Casals conducting, and with Rudolf Serkin at the keyboard. I studied chamber music in ensembles which included the most celebrated wind players in the world.

Marlboro gave me the musical standards and the tools I needed to reach a successful position within the music profession.

Rudolf Serkin's generosity and idealism are more impressive to me than ever, because I can appreciate better what personal sacrifices he made every summer for the sake of young musicians. He forsook a fortune in concert fees to spend his summers with players such as me.

Joseph Robinson, Marlboro Participant, 1969

Janice Meyerson, András Schiff, Luis Batlle, Daisy Newman. FACING PAGE Ralph Evans, Diane Monroe, Cecile Licad.

More Than Just Work and Inspiration

I was a participant at Marlboro from 1972 through 1976 . . . One of the first things that comes to mind as I scan those summers is the experience of preparing and performing quartets by Ravel, Bartok, Berg, and Schoenberg with Felix Galimir. These were all first performances for me, and they helped me prepare for the challenge of the string quartet career that I have subsequently pursued. I remember a post–season benefit performance of the Schumann Piano Quintet for the Marlboro Volunteer Fire Department. That was the one chance I had to collaborate with Rudolf Serkin, but as captain of the Dining Hall crew, I also had the privilege of telling Mr. Serkin, among others, which tables to set, serve, and clean up.

Marlboro did not only represent work and inspiration. It was fun. I remember innumerable trips to South Pond, the square dances, the film shows, dawdling in the Dining Hall after many meals to prolong the feeling of community that was hard to duplicate anywhere else. Sipping coffee while discussing Uruguayan history with Luis Batlle, comparing my generation's disenchantment and groping for new ideals with the malaise of the post–World War I generation in a discussion with Mr. Serkin, hanging out in the geodesic dome that served as a coffee shop every evening, I had a sense of belonging which mingled with the power of the music we all were working on, and with the natural beauty of the surroundings. This heady mixture always made it difficult to leave when the festival ended.

Eugene Drucker,
Marlboro Participant, 1972–76, 1993

Piano technician Franz Scheerer.

THE COMMUNITY

(Top left) Judy and Isidore Cohen, and friends, at a square dance. *(Top right)* Rudolf Serkin, Irene Serkin, and Martial Singher at a Marlboro picnic. *(Bottom)* Mischa Schneider, Samuel Rhodes, Philipp Naegele, Mieczyslaw Horszowski, and photographer Gjon Mili.

(Bottom right) Cellist Leslie Parnas.

An Underlying Affection

When the hall has been cleared of dishes and chairs and tables, the square dancing begins quickly—and violently. But there is none of the guests who is not equal to its pace. Even Rudolf Serkin. Even Rudolf Serkin who has played in the afternoon concert, who has helped to remove the chairs and tables, who has announced to those outside the beginning of the dancing. But that is the manner of Marlboro. It is not an admiration society. It is one in which esteem for one's fellow is a natural condition; in which there is an unusual capacity for joy; in which there is an underlying affection, with no self–consciousness, with no primary self–esteem, with no self–congratulation. It is an artless climate in which to hear music as music is.

When the dancing has been concluded, the participants stroll outside to farewells, to preparations for days immediately ahead, perhaps even for the next year. With grace and sincerity, but with no great to–do, Marlboro Music has completed all but one week of 25 years of authentic communion with music.

Frederick J. Kountz, Friend, 1976

Anton Kuerti, Bjoern Andreasson, Harry Zaratzian, and Camilla Doppmann rehearse as violinist Nancy Cirillo takes her turn on the dining hall crew.

(Right) Henry Nowak and son.

Unidentified child, Miriam Fried, Endel Kalam, Olga Iglesias.

Guest chef Alexander Schneider, Mieczyslaw Horszowski, Frank Salomon.

(Top) Irene Serkin is honored by the Marlboro Family. *(Bottom)* Felix Galimir (standing) at a celebratory dinner.

Unidentified man, Sylvia Rosenberg, Andre Aisenstadt, Anthony Checchia, and children at an honorary dinner for Mischa Schneider (sitting).

Napkin Throwing a Tradition

It's 6:30 on a Saturday evening. Dinner for the 60 participants in the Marlboro Music School and Festival, held in converted cow barn that Marlboro College calls its Dining Hall, is drawing to a close.

At this point at one of the world's high temples of chamber music, one would almost expect a devotional prayer from Artistic Director Rudolf Serkin, something to prepare body and soul for the upcoming public concert.

But a quick glance around the Dining Hall suggests something quite different; the only heads that are bowed are the ones that are ducking the flying paper napkins. Napkin throwing at the end of meals is a tradition at Marlboro, a tacit acknowledgement of the need for an emotional release following the many hours of rehearsal. Everyone participates, young and old alike.

Richard Riley,
The Sunday Republican, 1988

(Top) Paul Tortelier, Marcel Moyse, and children. *(Bottom)* Honoree Rudolf Serkin.

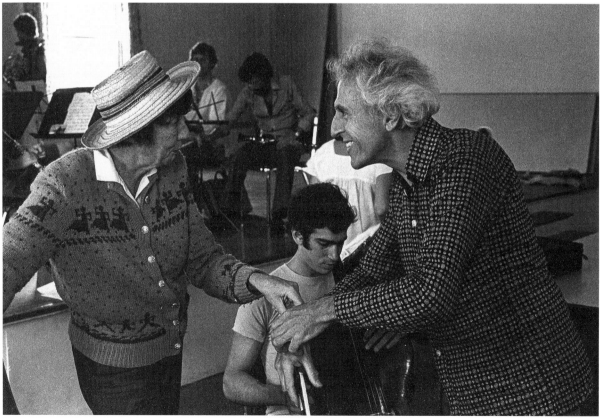

(Bottom) Madeline Foley, Jerry Grossman, Paul Tortelier.

(Right) Rudolf Serkin and friend.

Peter Serkin, Mieczyslaw Horszowski.

A Very Special Give and Take

This chance to live with, and not just play with, other talented musicians can benefit the performers as well, according to violist Samuel Rhodes, a participant who is now a member of the Juilliard Quartet. He says, "Chamber music requires a very special musical and human give and take. A community like Marlboro, where one lives, eats, talks and plays music in such a personal way, cannot help but have profound and lasting meaning for everyone who has the privilege of participating there."

Gretchen Becker, *Vermont Summer,*
Supplement to *The Bennington Banner*
and the *Brattleboro Reformer,* 1980

Unidentified, Carmit Zori, Luis Batlle, Serena Canino, Elena Canino.

Playing With Master Artists

... I was 19 when I first went there. The names of Rudolf Serkin, Pablo Casals, the Budapest Quartet, Mieczyslaw Horszowski were legendary to me and the chance to hear them was, I felt, the chance of a lifetime. The idea of actually playing with these masters and other great artists was to make an immeasurably strong impact on me. Before that, I had played chamber music, but mainly with schoolmates and friends; when we felt a piece was ready, we'd take it to a teacher—but I never had the opportunity to work on it from the beginning with an established artist. In Marlboro, I could do this with many pieces, and my first year was a kind of revelation: there were suddenly so many valid points of view and so many exciting ways to make music. Totally different ways. There was a new freedom in my life.

Things would be rehearsed with painstaking care, and not only Beethoven and Mozart. I remember doing quite a bit of modern music (Schoenberg's *Pierrot Lunaire*, Webern, Dallapiccola)—things I could do nowhere else because of the time and effort required from everybody.

Marlboro is also a place for lasting friendships. Bonds formed there, in a crucible of music–making, with music as a driving force behind them, have affected my entire life ...

Somehow, one always wants to define what it is that makes Marlboro so unique, so special—why is there such caring and love there? I think it has to do with its being Mr. Serkin's dream. ... His dedication to music is a dedication to humanity, its struggle and its victory. In the clear Vermont air, his dream breathes—may it go on forever.

Murray Perahia, Marlboro Participant, 1966–67, 1969, 1972

Kathy Lucktenberg, Young Uck Kim.

Living and Working Together

I realize what excites me so about this weekend goes beyond the music or any of the individuals. It is a sense of a whole community passionately absorbed in making something beautiful together.

What we all need, wherever we live, is a community like Marlboro. A community where we can be free from our isolation, where we are encouraged in creative activities we enjoy, and where we can cooperate instead of compete. As we drive out of town, I notice the sign on the road leading into Marlboro: CAUTION-MUSICIANS AT PLAY.

Betty Freidan, *McCall's,* 1971

(Top) Michelle Reed. FACING PAGE Rudolf Serkin, Mieczyslaw Horszowski, and Ruth Laredo studying Bach's *Concerto in D Minor for Three Pianos.*

OUTREACH, TOURS, AND RECORDINGS

Bringing the Results of Their Work
to a Larger Public

To a large extent, Marlboro was designed for the intellectual broadening of performers. Its public manifestations were incidental to that work: Columbia Masterworks' Music from Marlboro recordings brought the results of that work to a larger public. Remember, Marlboro concerts were small-building affairs, in which programs were not finally determined until the last moment, when works were selected out of a larger pool of music undergoing preparation. It takes a special kind of concertgoer, not a casual tourist or idle listener, to find such a way of doing things congenial.

Players active today who were influenced by happenings at Marlboro are really too numerous to mention. Every major string quartet and orchestra in the world has one or more, in some cases are composed of a majority, of Marlboro alumni/ae. Every third pianist, too, it seems ... performers of every possible musical persuasion have found in their two months of hardworking respite in southern Vermont a central core of ideals to carry them through the rest of the year and quite likely the rest of their lives.

It is most encouraging that Sony Classical, holder in due course of the treasures of CBS Masterworks, has seen fit to commemorate the fortieth anniversary of Marlboro with a genuine commercial commitment, in the form of at least fifteen CDs to be issued during the

present year, and who knows how many more to come. Not only are performances drawn from the large group of works recorded under the Music from Marlboro rubric for Columbia/CBS, but from the eighteen treasurable programs up to now available only by mail-order from Marlboro Music, and from a store of unrelated material that turns out to contain an impressive number of Marlboro Festival Orchestra performances led by Pablo Casals.

... Sony Classical's packaging includes personnel lists of the various configurations making up the "Marlboro Festival Orchestra" on these widely separated occasions. The string players' list reads like a roster of our leading chamber-music ensembles of the past two decades, unfortunately arranged alphabetically so that one cannot tell (as if it mattered) who is occupying what position within the band. Most of the winds and brass occupy positions of responsibility and prominence in first-rate North American orchestras. There are more than a few players in every category who have achieved solo careers.

... these five CD's document a generous sample of the Marlboro Festival's most consequential music-making, the findings of painstaking exploration. There's a goodly amount still to come ...

John Wiser, *Fanfare,* 1990

Emotional Commitment to the Essence of the Music

Early in its history, Marlboro established a connection with Mr. Serkin's label, Columbia Records. In addition, the festival set up the mail-order Marlboro Recording Society to issue other repertory, much of it presumably deemed "uncommercial" by Columbia (later CBS) Masterworks.

To celebrate Marlboro's 40th Anniversary, Sony Classical, which now owns the CBS Masterworks catalogue, is releasing 15 CD's of Marlboro performances, and 5 are at hand. Included is material previously available only through the Marlboro Society.

...A pairing of Bach's Orchestral Suites Nos. 2 and 3, from 1966 (SMK 45892), may come as a shock to young listeners. The interpretations embody an older, Romantic tradition in Bach performance. Mr. Casals does not elongate the dotted rhythms in the Overtures, for example, the way recent scholarship suggests. But what a sense of emotional commitment to the essence of the music emerges in these elegant and graceful performances.

A Schubert disk (SMK 45901) contains the oldest and newest performances thus far in the series ... The disk's major offering is a 1986 performance of Schubert's crowning master piece of chamber music, his String Quintet in C. The five players represent precisely the Marlboro performing tradition. Playing alongside Felix Galimir, one of the great musical figures of our time, are four of the brightest young musical talents of recent years ...

Each phrase is warmly embraced in total and intense involvement, and the Scherzo and finale have a robust and bracing vigor. The Marlboro performance affirms abiding and essential truths about the spiritual strength the institution breeds in its musicians.

Martin Bookspan,
The New York Times, 1990

Pablo Casals recorded the Bach Brandenburg Concertos and Orchestral Suites at Marlboro. OVERLEAF David Soyer with pianists Mieczyslaw Horszowski, Peter Serkin, and Rudolf Serkin, and Judith Serkin, in rehearsal of Bach's *Concerto in C for Three Pianos.*

Offering Additional Exposure

Recordings are made of all dress rehearsals and performances. These are for the School's archives and are used for study purposes by the resident musicians. These archives are permanently housed at the Library of Congress, and from them have come about ten 13-week series of one-hour and one-and-a-half hour radio programs that have offered additional exposure to Marlboro's young artists since 1968. Over 50 cities, large and small, have carried these broadcasts, enabling countless music lovers to hear the unusual repertoire and to share in the spirit of music-making that infuses the performances.

Belov, *American Record Guide,* May, 1980

(Top) Recording session of Brahms' *Liebeslieder Walzer* with Leon Fleisher, Rudolf Serkin, unidentified page-turner, Wayne Conner, Benita Valente, Marlene Kleinman Malas, Martial Singher. *(Bottom)* Scott Nickrenz, Recording & Archive Director Mischa Schneider, Felix Galimir, Masuko Ushioda, and Ronald Leonard listening to a dress rehearsal tape.

A Passionate Devotion to Chamber Music

Musicians from Marlboro is an offshoot of the summer music festival in Vermont, founded by the late violinist Adolf Busch, and pianist Rudolf Serkin, who still presides over it as guardian spirit and guide. The unique characteristic of the groups put together there, both for the summer session and the concert tours they undertake in the winter, is that students and teachers mingle in them so democratically that the listener is not aware of the distinction, except perhaps by the players' ages. What they all have in common is a passionate devotion to chamber music, and a high level of technical proficiency and musical commitment. The ensembles vary in size from three to eleven players and the programs offer a wide variety of works, some of them rarely heard and many in unusual combinations.

Strings, 1989

Musicians From Marlboro ensembles—Murray Perahia, Isidore Cohen, Nobuko Imai, and Timothy Eddy.

Resonates Throughout the World

What happens at Marlboro resonates throughout the international concert world. The Guarneri, Cleveland and Vermeer quartets were all born in Marlboro. For top–flight musicians like Harold Wright, first clarinetist of the Boston Symphony, and Myron Bloom, first French horn player in the Cleveland Orchestra, it was a perennial summer camp. In fact, it is hard to find a prominent American musician who hasn't spent at least one inspirational summer at Marlboro (the late Pablo Casals himself spent thirteen). For ten years, at the close of each summer, Marlboro has sent out chamber music groups to give about 50 "Music from Marlboro" concerts in places across the country where the unusual repertory of Marlboro music is unknown.

Hubert Saal, *Newsweek,* 1975

Felix Galimir, Ronald Copes, Miklos Perenyi, Richard Stoltzman, Kim Kashkashian, Nobuko Imai.

(Top) Yefim Bronfman, Shlomo Mintz, Paul Tobias, David Jolley. *(Bottom)* Jerry Grossman, Ira Weller, Bayla Keyes, Isidore Cohen, Judith Serkin, Rudolph Vrbsky.

Touring and Playing Experience

To the knowledgeable, Marlboro has always been a magic name. It is the town in Vermont where Rudolf Serkin, the pianist, and some of his well–known colleagues have gathered for many summers past to share their experience and wisdom with younger professional musicians and those who are ready for a professional career. "A fertile stew," was the mixed metaphor used by one participant to describe the assemblage of the gifted of all ages, for it has bred a number of famous ensembles such as the Guarneri String Quartet.

It also spawned a special project, the fruition of a long–held dream of Mr. Serkin's. This was Music from Marlboro, a series of mid–season tours by chamber groups formed during the summer.

Music from Marlboro had two aims, to bring chamber music masterpieces in the best possible performances to various communities and to provide touring and playing experience for young artists.

… One testifier is Paula Robison, the now celebrated flutist, who took part in five of the earliest tours. "They were my first tour situations," she says. "It was my first time in cities such as Philadelphia and Boston. I learned what it was like to drive through snow drifts in order to make a concert on time. I learned about hotels and hotel food, something that started me taking along health foods and bottles of vitamins. I learned about adjusting to different halls and different audience responses.

"Although Mr. Serkin, I believe, tried to put together ensembles that were congenial musically and personally, I think he also purposely did the opposite on occasion. It made it necessary for us to get along, to adjust and cooperate. Still, it was fun at the same time that it was educational. In a sense we were students yet we weren't in school. The spirit of Marlboro stayed with us in being together on the road."

Raymond Ericson,
The New York Times, 1977

Robert Routch, David Singer, Rudolph Vrbsky, Laurel Zucker, Michael Johns, Lynette Diers Cohen, Alexander Heller, Theodore Baskin, Stewart Newbold.

Performance is an Outlet but Not a Reason

It is a place to learn about music, but one finds here no teachers and no pupils. Marlboro's people do play concerts every weekend—1985's began yesterday—but all who come here are warned to harbor no rightful expectation of playing in any of them.

Marlboro is also a place for refreshment after the hard seasonal labor of the professional musician, yet no set of performers seem to work harder then the 60–odd individuals who gather here every year.

Marlboro is for the old and the young, the experienced and the novitiate, the starry soloist, the orchestra player and the student.

To rise above all these contradictions, suffice it to say that Marlboro is a place for making chamber music, nothing more and nothing less. The music is made privately and publicly, and when it is performed it comes almost as an afterthought—as a culmination of all the sharing that has gone on in Marlboro's carefully scheduled practice hours. Marlboro's audiences have learned to accept their secondary status—gladly, it seems, judging from the sold–out houses at the 668–seat theater here. Most listeners come not knowing what or whom

they will hear. Programs are decided a day in advance.

There is method, not caprice, in this last-minute scheduling. Indeed, perhaps Marlboro's most impressive administrative feature is its ability to plan with care and yet change these plans as the moment dictates. Concert life, in other words, dictates that X will play Y on the day of Z—regardless. Marlboro, on the other hand, says, "We'll practice a lot of music and see what is ready."

If a piece needs one week or seven, it will be pursued to the satisfaction of its performers and then played for all. If the performers do not gel gracefully, if interpretation reaches an impasse, it will be dropped. The burden of deadline has been removed and the burden that replaces it is one of musical quality—which is to be pursued outside the normal time constraints of the music business. "Performance," say its organizers, "is an outlet but not a reason" for all that happens here. The enormous respect Marlboro seems to evoke from musicians is largely for this fact.

Bernard Holland,
The New York Times, 1985

Richard Stoltzman, Andre-Michel Schub, Ronald Leonard, Felix Galimir. FACING PAGE Naomi Katz, Ulrich Eichenauer, Pamela Frank, Julia Lichten, Scott St. John, Gustav Rivinius, Ivan Chan, Eric Grossman.

Learning Tenacity of Purpose

I was fortunate to participate in two Music from Marlboro tours. . . . On the first tour with Isidore Cohen I was struck by Izzy's phenomenal energy. We were playing the Schubert Cello Quintet with all those nasty octaves for the two violins, and before *every single* concert Izzy would be lurking near my dressing room, waiting to ambush me into yet another rehearsal of those damned octaves. This behavior did not cease or in any way diminish as the tour progressed. The fact that Izzy hit them in every concert made not a whit of difference. From this I learned tenacity of purpose.

Bayla Keyes, Marlboro Participant, 1977–79

András Schiff, Hiroko Yajima, Gary Hoffman.

Doing it Right Remains a Necessity

It is a dream . . . that will remain with a lot of Marlboro musicians after they leave here this summer and go out to face the fall season, the dream that musical perform-ance is not always subject to the demands of volume and velocity. Also offered is a glimmer of hope that the chase for success, stardom and money has not wholly overwhelmed the music world. Maybe doing it right is still an option—and maybe making the sacrifices necessary to do it right remains a necessity.

Bernard Holland, *Vermont Magazine,* 1992

Felix Galimir, Kwang-Wu Kim, Matthias Naegele, Evan Wilson.

Creating a Life-long Commitment

My memories of Marlboro are a jumble of many different things—musical and social, very profound and very silly—and I think it's accurate to describe the place as profound one minute and silly the next because the intensity with which we spend so many hours in a day struggling towards absolute integrity in our music-making has to be relieved by some completely opposing activity—like reconstructing someone's bedroom on the roof.

. . . of enormous importance was my first encounter with the composers of the Second Viennese School, working on the Berg Opus 3 String Quartet with Felix Galimir. Felix (and I still can only call him this on paper or when he's not in the room!) not only made this new language utterly clear and comprehensible, but created in me, and I believe in everyone who was able to work with him, a lifelong commitment to this exciting period of musical history.

Particularly for all the female string players (and this is *not* a sexist remark!), playing with Pina Carmirelli is a total joy as well as a shining ideal. Her passion and, most of all, her power in communicating it is some-thing to really aspire to, especially in contrast with her gentleness away from the violin.

And finally there was Mischa Schneider, to whom I was very attached. He was an opinionated, devoted, tough, and loving presence. . . . He was our keen critic at all dress rehearsals after which we would squeeze into the recording room with him, congregate at his feet, and he'd tell us everything that wasn't working and praise what was—and he was always right, and you can bet we'd have whatever was wrong fixed by concert time. I always looked forward to the post-mortems too; slipping into the recording room again, usually to get a satisfied smile and a kiss on the head or sometimes to be told "well, it still didn't work," but still getting a kiss on the head. I miss Mischa very much.

But I think that is really the essence of Marlboro—learning that success doesn't really exist and isn't the point; that having that indefinable "more" to work towards has to be the motivation for continuing to make music.

Ida Levin,
Marlboro Participant, 1981–84

Pina Carmirelli.

(Top) Rudolf Serkin, Bruno Canino. *(Bottom)* Administrators Anthony Checchia and Frank Salomon with Rudolf Serkin.

A *Diamond in the Rough*

A motorist on southern Vermont's Rte. 9 at dusk on a Saturday night might well miss the few unobtrusive signs to Marlboro Music. Only after winding down some three miles of narrow road lined with red barns and 18th Century houses and tall trees do you finally encounter a sign reading, "Caution: Musicians at Play."

Suffice it to say, glitz is not the style at the Marlboro Music Festival, as the chamber music–filled summer of practice sessions, concerts and more practice sessions is sometimes called. Though tickets to its concerts sell out weeks in advance, and though hundreds of classical artists vie for 60 or so spots as participants each summer, after almost four decades of existence, the festival remains very much a diamond in the rough.

The message behind the plain physical appointments is clear: It is the music that matters. The festival's obscure setting and unpretentious trappings belie its importance in giving gifted musicians, young and old, the kind of musical experiences that conservatories generally do not provide. And through the years many thousands of listeners . . . have been the almost incidental beneficiaries of Marlboro's unusual approach to music–making.

James Schwartz, *Newsday,* 1989

Philipp Naegele, Camilla Doppmann.

PARTICIPANTS

Marlboro Music School and Festival Participants

PIANO

Philip Aaberg
Rieko Aizawa
Judith Alstadter
Kenneth Amada
Ronit Amir
Mitchell Andrews
Ruslana Antonowicz
Igor Ardašev
Lydia Artymiw
Vovka Ashkenazy
Richard Aslanian
Dickran Atamian
Edward Auer
Emanuel Ax
Paul Badura-Skoda
Thomas Bagwell
Nerine Barrett
Luis Batlle
Charlotte Behrendt
Martin Berkofsky
Boris Berman
Barbara Blegen
Bonnie Bogle
Ossie Borosh
Yefim Bronfman
Kathryn Brown
Stephanie Brown
John Browning
Judith Burganger
John Buttrick
Bruno Canino
Seth Carlin
Jeffrey Chappell
Katherine Chi
Chia Chou
Van Cliburn
Evelyne Crochet
Tan Crone
Katharina Heinz David
Laura De Fusco
William Doppman
Barry Douglas
David Effron
Carol Eshak
Virginia Rubottom Eskin
Lorraine Falberg
Meira Farkas
Arthur Fennimore
Esther Fernandez
Monica Feuermann
Rudolf Firkušný
George Fishoff
Leon Fleisher

Julian Foster
Lily Fox
Malcolm Frager
Claude Frank
Robert Freeman
Yukino Fujiwara
Shirley X. Gabis
Roswitha Gediga
David Golub
Richard Goode
Alexander Goor
Judith Gordon
Gary Graffman
David Gross
Paul Gulda
Marian Hahn
Derek Han
Tong-Il Han
Wu Han
Andrew Heath
Ann Heiligman
George Henry
Ivette Hernandez
Judith Hirsch
Ian Hobson
Paige Roberts Hoffman
Lorin Hollander
Patricia Hopkins
William Horn
Mieczyslaw Horszowski
Naoyuki Inoue
Diedre Irons
Roglit Ishay
Eugene Istomin
Judith Jaimes
Li Jian
Veronica Jochum
David Johnston
Gilbert Kalish
Lilian Kallir
Anita Katchen
Constance Keene
Dukju Kim
Kwang-Wu Kim
Walter Klien
Dina Koston
Edith Kraft
Anton Kuerti
Sara Laimon
Ruth Laredo
Jacob Lateiner
Theodore Lettvin
Ernest Levenstein
Beth Levin
David Levine

Dena Levine
James Levine
Frank Levy
Cecile Licad
Eleanor Lipkin
Seymour Lipkin
Eugene List
Maria Lopez-Vito
Thomas Lorango
Jerome Lowenthal
Joyce Lowry
Lee Luvisi
Alan Mandel
Stephen Manes
Wolfgang Manz
Alan Marks
Martha Masséna
Robert McDonald
Jeremy Menuhin
Marilyn Meyer
Bertrand Molia
Maria Mosca
Frederick Moyer
Peter Nagy
Marilyn Neeley
Toby Nevis
Erika Nickrenz
Michael Oelbaum
Hilda Offermann
Atsuko Ohori
Ursula Oppens
Christopher O'Riley
Peter Orth
Cristina Ortiz
Lois Carole Pachucki
Zaidee Parkinson
Patricia Parr
Andrea Passigli
Rebecca Penneys
Murray Perahia
Beverly Phillips
Sally Pinkas
Alain Planès
Boris Poliakine
Eloise Polk
Walter Ponce
Joy Pottle
Patricia Prattis
Stephen Prutsman
Hannah Prydatkevytch
Cynthia Raim
Joel Rice
James Richman
John Ritter
Jerome Rose

Irene Rosenberg
Renata Rosenblatt
Lilli Bohnke Rosenthal
Adrian Ruiz
Joel Sachs
Samuel Sanders
Alicia Schachter
András Schiff
Mark Schneider
Paul Schoenfield
André-Michel Schub
Irene Schreier
Marilyn Schultz
Kathryn Selby
Peter Serkin
Rudolf Serkin
Daniel Shapiro
Henry Shapiro
Zola Mae Shaulis
Paul Shaw
Thomas Shepard
Craig Sheppard
Leonard Shure
Jeffrey Siegel
Alexander Slobodyanik
Shirley Smethen
Lawrence Smith
Debbie Sobol
Ignat Solzhenitsyn
Claudette Sorel
Susan Starr
Victor Steinhardt
Cheryl Stern
Judith Stillman
Richard Syracuse
Natasha Tadson
Kiyoko Takeuti
Marc Taslitt
Etsuko Tazaki
Nina Tichman
Margaret Tolson
Friederike Trauer
Gilles Tremblay
Kwong-Kwong Tung
Ronald Turini
Mitsuko Uchida
June Urquhart
Dénes Várjon
Stefan Vladar
Ralph Votapek
Diane Walsh
Vivian Hornik Weilerstein
Alan Weiss
Piero Weiss
Gloria Whitney

James Wolfe
Elizabeth Wright
Roxana Wruble
Mikhail Yanovitsky
Marion Zarzeczna
Idith Zvi

HARPSICHORD

Mary Alderdice
Maryse Carlin
Suzanne Cleverdon
Robert Conant
Kenneth Cooper
Paul Fayko
Eiji Hashimoto
Gregory Hayes
Tonu Kalam
Mark Kroll
Robert Levin
Robert Merfeld
Jens Nygaard
Doris Ornstein
Edith Picht-Axenfeld
Charles Sherman
Andrew Willis
Wendy Young

VIOLIN

Salvatore Accardo
Sanford Allen
Dorothy Alpert
Christian Altenburger
Bjoern Andreasson
Goesta Andreasson
Leah Arner
Shmuel Ashkenasi
Liliana Ciulei Atanasiu
Norma Auzin
Charles Avsharian
Christel Baillie
Dorothy Bales
Gabriel Banat
Elena Barere
Margaret Batjer
Joshua Bell
Jeanne Benjamin
Krista Bennion
Yehonatan Berick
Lori Courant Berkowitz
Wallace Berul
Sophie Besançon
Vera Beths
Ida Bieler
Paul Biss
Carol Block
Emmanuelle Boisvert

Norbert Brainin
Jacqueline Brand
Elizabeth Burckhardt
Barbara Burgdorf
Adolf Busch
James Buswell
Serena Canin
Pina Carmirelli
Charles Castleman
Jesse Ceci
Corey Cerovsek
Ivan Chan
Robert Chen
Lynn Chang
Olivier Charlier
Stephanie Chase
Leland Chen
Catherine Cho
Young-Mi Cho
Nancy Chute
Nancy Cirillo
Isidore Cohen
Richard Collins
Ronald Copes
Stephen Copes
Dorothy Ann Cramer
Miranda Cuckson
John Dalley
Antonino David
Alvaro De Granda
Margarita Delacorte
William de Pasquale
Ralph De Souza
Robert Dew
Glenn Dicterow
Sarah Dines
Robert Dressler
Eugene Drucker
Marilyn Dubow
Suzanne Dyner
Sigrún Edvaldsdóttir
Oscar Ekberg
Ralph Evans
Virginia Farmer
Leonard Felberg
Sheila Fiekowsky
Karin-Regina Florey
Pamela Frank
Catherine French
Miriam Fried
Eric Friedman
Martin Friedmann
Mayuki Fukuhara
Gregory Fulkerson
Felix Galimir
Saschko Gawriloff
Gudrun Gay
Sylvie Gazeau

Pamela Gearhart
Joseph Genualdi
Carroll Glenn
Maynard Goldman
Cora Gordon
Marc Gottlieb
Barbara Govatos
Nisanne Graff
Endre Granat
Deborah Greenebaum
Roland Greutter
Alan Grishman
Eric Grossman
Bira Haas
Diana Halprin
Laura Hamilton
Julius Hegyi
Mary Crowder Hess
Grete Hirsch
Momoko Horigome
Yuzuko Horigome
Lynn Horner
Nai-Yuan Hu
Bin Huang
Mark Huggins
Peggy James
Piotr Janowski
Nora Joffe
Renée Jolles
Leila Josefowicz
Helen Journet
Eugene Kahn
Lilla Kalman
Yukiko Kamei
Juliette Kang
Tomoko Kato
Naomi Katz
Ani Kavafian
Bayla Keyes
Benny Kim
Chee-Yun Kim
Hyunmi Kim
Young-Nam Kim
Young Uck Kim
Christopher Kimber
Tiberius Klausner
Melissa Kleinbart
Veronica Knittel
Kenji Kobayashi
Victoria Kobayashi
Robert Koff
Rudolf Kolisch
Walter Koppleman
Henryk Kowalski
Vera Vaidman Krasovsky
Takumi Kubota
Sarah Kwak
Jaime Laredo

Elaine Lee
Kyung-Sun Lee
Ronan Lefkowitz
Oswald Lehnert
Hou Lei
Kathleen Lenski
Andrea Bircsak Leung
Ida Levin
Myron Levitsky
Amnon Levy
Samuel Levy
Mei-Chen Liao
Klaus Liepman
Lise Liepman
S. Anna Lim
Cho Liang Lin
Charles-André Linale
Mauro Loguercio
Richard Luby
Sergiu Luca
Kathy Lucktenberg
Si-Hon Ma
Frances Magnes
Michelle Makarski
Sidney Mann
Robert Mark
Ulrike-Anima Mathé
Yoko Matsuda
Kerry McDermott
Pierre Menard
Geoffrey Michaels
Thomas Michalak
Shlomo Mintz
Sonya Monosoff
Diane Monroe
David Montagu
Greg Moore
Blanche Honegger Moyse
Gilda Muhlbauer
Viktoria Mullova
Takahiro Muroya
Philipp Naegele
Sachiko Nakajima
Yoshiko Nakura
Lucy Nedzel
Margo Neuhof
Ronald Oakland
Hirono Oka
Elmar Oliveira
Jennifer Orchard
Junko Ota
Igor Ozim
Michaela Modjeska Paetsch
Tedi Papavrami
Chul-In Park
Laura Park
Edith Peinemann
Pasquale Pellegrino

Oscar Pereira
Jane Peters
Daniel Phillips
Todd Phillips
Michael Rabin
Max Rabinovitsj
Joseph Rabushka
Toni Rapport
Florika Remetier
Barbara Renner
Gerardo Ribeiro
Evelyn Riesman
Mary Kay Robinson
Jerome Rosen
Sylvia Rosenberg
Julie Rosenfeld
Lara St. John
Scott St. John
Peter Salaff
Gino Sambuco
Leonard Samuels
Alexander Schneider
Gottfried Schneider
Mona Schoen
Ernestine Briesmeister
    Schor
Joseph Schor
Michel Schwalbe
Florence Schwartz
Berl Senofsky
Irene Busch Serkin
Philip Setzer
Liba Shacht
Leslie Shank
Robin Sharp
Eyal Shiloach
Yuuko Shiokawa
Helen Shklar
Carol Sindell
Deborah Singer
Alan Sklar
Laurie Smukler
Herbert Sorkin
Barbara Sorlien
Marylou Speaker
Annie Steiger
Mark Steinberg
Diana Steiner
Arnold Steinhardt
Richard Sterba
James Stern
Mitchell Stern
Lucy Chapman Stoltzman
Bruno Straumann
Takaoki Sugitani
Hidetaro Suzuki
Andrew Svilokos
Ian Swensen

Joseph Swensen
Susan Synnestvedt
Naoko Tanaka
Christian Tetzlaff
Elizabeth Titus
Yan Pascal Tortelier
Jon Toth
Michael Tree
Mari Tsumura
Ling Tung
Janet Kendall Turkovic
Asako Urushihara
Masuko Ushioda
Erno Valašek
Teresa Vannin
Patricia Grimes Vas Dias
Sandor Vegh
Kai Vogler
I-Fu Wang
Zheng-Rong Wang
Julia Watson
Hazel Weems
Annette Wegiel
Donald Weilerstein
Marcia Weinfeld
Lisa Weiss
Elaine Weldon
Steven Wernick
Shirley Williams
Hiroko Yajima
Yosef Yankelev
Ayako Yoshida
David Zafer
Marion Zarzeczna
Julia Zaustinsky
Peter Zazofsky
Thomas Zehetmair
Zvi Zeitlin
Gladys Zera
Qian Zhao
Carmit Zori

VIOLA

Misha Amory
Steven Ansell
Fausto Anzelmo
Toby Appel
Lotte Bamberger
Daniel Barrach
Sydney Beck
Alisa Belzer
Vinciane Béranger
Lori Courant Berkowitz
Hatto Beyerle
Luigi Alberto Bianchi
Paul Biss
Virginia Blakeman

Sarah-Jane Bradley
Mimi Bravar
Lila Brown
Matthias Buchholz
Judith Busbridge
Annie Chang
Choong-Jin Chang
William Chute
Nancy Cirillo
Sarah Clarke
Caroline Louise Coade
Sarah Cossum
Nina Courant
Wayne Crouse
Sidney Curtiss
Rodney Dennis
Ellen dePasquale
Roberto Díaz
Karen Dreyfus
James Dunham
Ulrich Eichenauer
Nancy Ellis
Gertrude Emery
Csába Erdélyi
Nina Falk
Marie Finckel
Richard Foodim
Daniel Foster
Sylvie Gazeau
Geraldine Gee
Bruno Giuranna
Jacob Glick
John Graham
Charles Griffin
Victoria Gunn
John Hamilton
Mary Hammann
Jennie Hansen
Miriam Hartman
Raphael Hillyer
Claudia Hofert
Toby Hoffman
Hsin-Yun Huang
Christof Huebner
Matthew Hunter
Seymour Illions
Nobuko Imai
Theodore Israel
Maxine Johnson
Eugene Kahn
Endel Kalam
Lilla Kalman
Kim Kashkashian
Martha Strongin Katz
Naomi Katz
Isaac Kaufman
Yoshiko Kawamoto
Hazel Kerlin

Myra Kestenbaum
Kay Knudsen
Boris Kroyt
Lee Lane
Jaime Laredo
Doris Lederer
Pierre Lenert
Caroline Levine
Myron Levitsky
Bernard Linden
Hui Liu
Leslie Malowany
Raymond Marsh
Patricia McCarty
Donald McInnes
Jorge Mester
Susie Mészáros
Catherine Metz
Geoffrey Michaels
Gaetan Molieri
Sonya Monosoff
Raymond Montoni
Rainer Moog
Linda Moss
Blanche Honegger Moyse
Katherine Murdock
Philipp Naegele
Ah Ling Neu
Paul Neubauer
Margot Neuhof
Scott Nickrenz
Heiichiro Ohyama
Massimo Paris
Arrigo Pelliccia
Guillermo Perich
Cynthia Phelps
Elizabeth Phillips
Glenna Pohly
Madeline Prager
Karie Prescott
Hannah Prydatkevytch
Dorian Rence
Rhoda Rhea
Samuel Rhodes
Lesley Robertson
Carla-Maria Rodrigues
Ellen Rose
Toni Riley
Jerome Rosen
Arthur Royval
Scott St. John
Eckart Schloifer
William Schoen
Ernestine Briesmeister
    Schor
Midhat Serbagi
Irene Busch Serkin
Jack Shapiro

Minna Shklar
Benjamin Simon
Meredith Snow
Herbert Sorkin
Marylou Speaker
Arnold Steinhardt
Victor Stern
Benjamin Solow
Lucille Taylor
Steven Tenenbom
Marcus Thompson
Karen Trampler
Walter Trampler
Michael Tree
Ling Tung
Thomas Turner
Francis Tursi
Karen Tuttle
Asdís Valdimarsdóttir
Robert Verebes
Robert Vernon
Ilona Vukovic
Geraldine Lamboley
   Walther
Ira Weller
Barbara Westphal
Ralph Wheelock
Evan Wilson
Barbara Wright
Donald Wright
Phillip Ying
Harry Zaratzian
Bernard Zaslav
Tabea Zimmermann

VIOLA DA GAMBA

Judith Davidoff
Richard Taruskin

CELLO

Pablo Casals *(Special Guest)*
Gianna Abondolo
Gerald Appleman
Fortunato Arico
Ellen Marie Arrigo
Christopher von Baeyer
Eric von Baeyer
Grace Bahng
Alexander Baillie
Marcia Barbour
Melissa Barnard
Eric Bartlett
Vivian Barton
Pierre Basseux
Lorin Bernsohn
Lowri Blake

Ulrich Boeckheler
Ramon Bolipata
Terry Braverman
John Brockway
Melissa Brooks
Denis Brott
Regula Burckhardt
Herman Busch
Colin Carr
Nathan Chaikin
Paul Cheifetz
Rosalyn Clarke
David Cole
Rohini Coomara
Roberta Cooper
Christopher Costanza
Charles Curtis
Robie Brown Dan
Judith Davidoff
Joanna De Keyser
Henri Demarquette
William De Rosa
Rohan De Saram
Andrés Díaz
Burton Dines
Steven Doane
Camilla Doppman
Zon Eastes
Timothy Eddy
Eugene Eicher
André Emelianoff
Jules Eskin
Georg Faust
Rafael Figueroa
Mileva Fialova
Rocco Filippini
David Finckel
George Finckel
Michael Flaksman
Madeline Foley
Pamela Frame
Barbara Fryer
Hélène Gagné
Rudolf Gleissner
John Goberman
Ann Goodman
Johannes Goritzki
Michael Grebanier
Leo Grinhauz
Jerry Grossman
Michael Haber
Matt Haimovitz
Bonnie Hampton
Yehuda Hanani
Jiří Hanousek
Lynn Harrell
Benar Heifetz
Klaus Heitz

Stephen Herrold
Takeichiro Hirae
Desmond Hoebig
Annabelle Hoffman
Gary Hoffman
Henri Honegger
Janet Horvath
Jay Humeston
Thomas Igloi
Ko Iwasaki
Käthe Jarka
Verna Jarnot
Claus Kanngiesser
Paul Katz
Yeesun Kim
James Kreger
Joel Krosnick
Toshio Kuronuma
Lisa Lancaster
Jennifer Langham
Ronald Leonard
Laurence Lesser
Arthur Lessing
Amy Levine
Julia Lichten
Katja Linfield
Ronald Lipscomb
Yo Yo Ma
Stefan Machlup
Robert Maine
Mischa Maisky
Hampton Mallory
Joanne Manuuel
Robert Martin
Anne Martindale
Michael Mathews
Donald McCall
Charles McCracken
Melissa Meell
Thomas Metzger
Alain Meunier
Robert Miller
Theodore Mook
Matthias Naegele
George Neikrug
Hai-Ye Ni
Lawrence Oncley
Margaret Ostin
Siegfried Palm
Leslie Parnas
Miklós Perényi
Albert Petillo
Zvi Plesser
Jean-Guihen Queyras
Fred Raimi
Kari-Lise Ravnan
Dorothy Reichenberger
Gabor Rejto

Peter Rejto
Michael Reynolds
Robert Ripley
Gustav Rivinius
Sharon Robinson
Judith Rosen
Marcy Rosen
Nathaniel Rosen
Peter Rosenfeld
Michael Rudiakow
Toby Saks
Sara Sant'Ambrogio
George Saslow
Adam Satinsky
Peter Schenkman
Mischa Schneider
Angela Schwartz
Astrid Schween
Peter Seidenberg
Gertrude Seifman
Judith Serkin
Sophie Shao
John Sharp
Richard Sher
Paula Skolnick
Clarke Slater
Brinton Smith
Gayle Smith
Lloyd Smith
Wilhelmina Smith
Jeffrey Solow
Raphael Sommer
David Soyer
Jonathan Spitz
Evalyn Steinbock
Frances Steiner
Markus Stocker
Francesco Strano
Peter Stumpf
Wendy Sutter
Robert Sylvester
Nobuko Takeuti
Mark Tanner
Karen Thimann
Paul Tobias
Paul Tortelier
Shirley Trepel
Bion Tsang
Yuan Tung
David Vanderkooi
Jan Vogler
Wendy Warner
Paul Watkins
Sallie WeMott
Peter Wiley
Dmitry Yablonsky
Sofia Zappi
Hillel Zori

DOUBLE BASS

Edward Arian
Raymond Benner
Gino Biondo
Alan Birnbaum
Steve Brewster
William Burns
Joseph Carver
James Clute
Timothy Cobb
Marji Danilow
Carolyn Davis
Walter Freimanis
Robert Goodlett
Donald Hermanns
Samuel Hollingsworth
Julius Ilku
George Koukly
Gail Kruvand
John Kulowitch
Julius Levine
Bernard Lieberman
Peter Lloyd
Marc Marder
Susan Matthew
Edgar Meyer
Orin O'Brien
Shelley Saxon
Neil Stannard
Nicolas Tsolainos
Elizabeth Turner
Barbara Wilson
Guillermo Xucla

HARP

Carol Baum
Georganne Cassat
Carol Crosby
Margarita Csonka
Marcella DeCray
Deborah Fleisher
Alice Giles
Suzanne Handel
Ann Hobson
Yolanda Kondonassis
Marcela Kozikova
Heidi Lehwalder
Karen Lindquist
Jude Mollenhauer
Nanette Norton
Janet Putnam
Rita Tursi
Frances Cohen Woodhams
Moya Wright
Elyse Yockey
Naoko Yoshino

GUITAR

Javier Calderon
Fred Hand
Fredric J. Lehrman
Bill Matthews
Emanuele Segre
Stanley Silverman
David Starobin

MANDOLIN

Jacob Glick
Peter Press

LUTE

Stanley Charkey
Edward Flower
Chris Williams

ACCORDION

Jacqueline Hofto

FLUTE

Robert Aitken
Patricia Albinson
Edith Anthony
Ellen Marie Arrigo
Aram Bedrossian
Jacob Berg
Julia Bogorad
Amy Borman
Paul Boyer

Annabelle Caner
Vincent Cavalli
Kathleen Chastain
Ira Clark
Patricia Cobb
Joseph Cohen (Joseph Cobert)
Mardele Combs
Joan Cornell
Wayne Crebo
Nancy Dalley
Michel Debost
Eve Dickens
Joanne Dickinson
Rose Marie Dinner
Paul Dunkel
Bart Feller
Nicholas Fiore
Lois Friedlander
Jillian Frisch
Katharine Frost
Georgetta Gatto
Dejan Gavria
Laura Gilbert
Bernard Goldberg
Caroline Grimes
Ornulf Gulbransen
Viviana Guzmán
Ann Harnsberger
Margie Lee Johnson
Harold Jones
Francine Jupp
Kay Kennedy
Jean Kershaw
Chang-Kook Kim
Toshiko Kohno

Karl Kraber
Renée Krimsier
Eleanor Lawrence
Jean-Maurice Ledoux
Carol Lee
Barbara Leibundguth
Judith Ann Lyons
Mary Macomber
Marilyn Martin
Natalie Martin
Nicole Martin
Peter Martin
Judith Mendenhall
Patricia Miller
Soichi Minegishi
William Montgomery
Gretchen Moore
Susan Morris
Louis Moyse
Marcel Moyse
Christine Nield
Alex Ogle
Martin Orenstein
Phyllis Parker
Michael Parloff
Barbara Peterson
Marina Piccinini
Gertrude Pinion
Christine Reed
Odile Renault
Darlene Rhodus
Paula Robison
Rhoda Ross
Susan Rotholz
Judith Schenkman
Marguerite Serkin

(Left) Judith Serkin. *(Right)* David Levine, Renée Siebert.

Nan Sharp
Renée Siebert
Felix Skowronek
Carol Spiegel
Susan Stewart
Margaret Strum
Barbara Todd
Erich Toeplitz
Dorothy Turnipseed
Ann A. Unterecker
Marge Veleta
Carole Wang
Marjorie Wiener
Carol Wincenc
Barbara Worthley
Ruth Wurster Wright
Richard Wyszynski
Jane Young
Laurel Zucker

OBOE

Leonard Arner
Robert Atherholt
Theodore Baskin
William Bennett
Melvin Berman
Neil Black
Lon Bussell
James Caldwell
Peter Christ
Roger Cole
Randall Cook
Dianne Copelon
Matthew Dine
Elaine Douvas
John Ferrillo
Alfred Genovese
Kathleen Golding
Ann Greenawalt
Kathryn Greenbank
Patricia Grignet

Fred Gruenebaum
Georges Louis Haas
Michael Henoch
Stevens Hewitt
Robbie Lynn Hunsinger
Scott Janusch
Alex Klein
Cynthia Koledo
Charles Kuskin
John Mack
Janet Mascaro
Sharon Meekins
Bruill Moore
DeVere Moore
Eric Olson
Leslie Poindexter
Wayne Rapier
Deborah Reich
Mildred Remis
Gerard Reuter
Ronald Richards
Joseph Robinson
Samuel Robinson
Ronald Roseman
Louis Rosenblatt
Michael Rosenberg
Harry Sargous
Earl Schuster
Louise Scribner
Harry Shulman
Jacques Simard
Rheta Smith
Elizabeth (Betsy) Starr
Raymond Still
Daniel Stolper
Laila Storch
Linda Strommen
Seizo Suzuki
Laurence Thorstenberg
Joseph Turner
Humphrey Vas Dias
Stephen Vise

Allan Vogel
Rudolph Vrbsky
Robert Walters
Lois Wann
Randall Wolfgang
Richard Woodhams
Marilyn Zupnik

ENGLISH HORN

Janet Rarick

CLARINET

John Adams
Laura Ardan
David Bellman
Stuart Best
Eduard Brunner
Carmine Campione
Ronald Chandler
Ron Chen-Zion
Susan Cogan
Frank Cohen
Lawrence Combs
James Corwin
Andrew Crisanti
Emery Davis
Ronald Dennis
Eli Eban
Frank Ell
Margaret Ewing
Anthony Fulginiti
John Fullam
John Genovese
Robert Genovese
Yehuda Gilad
Janet Greene
William Hilferty
Cheryl Hill
William Huntington
Steven Jackson
Fred Jacobowitz
Mark Karlin
John Koljonen
David Krakauer
Jack Kreiselman
William Kushner
Richard Lesser
Todd Levy
Elsa Ludewig
John Lynes
Charles MacLeod
Daniel McKelway
Donald Montanaro
Stewart Newbold
Orit Orbach
Todd Darren Palmer

Thomas Peterson
Richard Pickar
Vito Platamone
Kenneth Radnofsky
Albert Regni
Paul Riesman
Charles Russo
Shannon Scott
David Singer
Ethan Sloane
Alan Solomon
Jo-Ann Sternberg
Don Stewart
Richard Stoltzman
Virginia Stroh
Theresa Tunnicliff
Joaquin Valdepeñas
John Van Bockern
Richard Waller
Michael Webster
Nancy Wenk
Harold Wright
William Wrzesien
Bernard Yannotta
John Bruce Yeh
Michele Zukovsky

BASSET HORN

Jane Hamborsky

SAXOPHONE

Lynn Klock
Harvey Pittel
Kenneth Radnofsky
Sigurd Rascher

BASSOON

Fred Alston
Eric Arbiter
Jane Cardwell
Anthony Checchia
Isabelle Clore
Lynette Diers Cohen
Gerald Corey
Rachel Davis
Steven Dibner
Vincent Ellin
Thomas Elliott
Joel Feinglass
Michael Finn
Bernard Garfield
Nancy Goeres
Clelia Goldings
George Goslee
Arthur Grossman

Madeline Foley, Luis Batlle.

Alexander Heller
Charles Holdeman
Benjamin Kamins
Matthew Karr
Joyce Kelley
Nicholas Kilburn
Sylvia Deutscher Kushner
Donald MacCourt
Stephen Maxym
David McGill
Christopher Millard
Kenneth Moore
Robert Moore
Kenneth Munday
Ryohei Nakagawa
Isabelle Plaster
Stefanie Przybylska
Richard Ranti
Mordechai Rechtman
Patricia Rogers
Sidney Rosenberg
Matthew Ruggiero
Daniel Sagarman
Peter Schoenbach
Sol Schoenbach
William Scribner
Roland Small
Jane Taylor
Mark Timmerman
Muneo Tozawa
Milan Turkovic
Kim Walker
William Winstead
Thomas Woodhams

CONTRABASSOON

Donald Bravo
Donald MacCourt
Stephen Young

HORN

David Allan
Carol Bacon
John Barrows
Kendall Betts
Myron Bloom
Robert Bonnevie
Arthur Brooks
E. Scott Brubaker
Janet Cardwell
Earl Chapin
Christine Chapman
Daniel Cowan
Christopher Earnest
Victoria Eisen
Horace Fitzpatrick

Robert Fries
Ralph Froelich
Martha Glaze
Daniel Grabois
Robin Graham
Tully Hall
Thomas Holden
Paul Ingraham
Michael Johns
Robert Johnson
David Jolley
Chris Komer
Julie Landsman
Ib Lanzky-Otto
Jane Lowenstein
Judith Mackey
Richard Mackey
Arnold Mascaro
Thomas McAninch
Bruce McLellan
Marie-Luise Neunecker
Barbara Oldham
Karl Pituch
Ralph Pottle
Samuel Ramsey
Michelle Reed
Meir Rimon
Stewart Rose
Donald Rosenberg
Lloyd Rosevear
Robert Routch
Susan Sabin
Stephen Seiffert

John Serkin
John David Smith
Richard Solis
Martin Webster
Shirley Ann Weekley
David Wetherill

TRUMPET

Carl Albach
Ronald K. Anderson
Donald Bernstein
Howard M. Birnbaum
Glenn Bowling
Phyllis Cannatta
Allen Dean
Christian Ferrari
John Glasel
Raphael Glaser
Martin Goldbaum
Judith Higgins
Charles Hois
Fred Holmgren
Boyde Hood
David Jandorf
Gilbert Johnson
Larry Knopp
Joseph Koplin
Eugene Kuntz
Stuart Laughton
Albert Ligotti
Rodney Mack
Wayne J. du Maine

Rob Roy McGregor
Fred Mills
Robert Nagel
Henry Nowak
Louis Opalesky
Frank Ostrowski
Nedo Pandolfi
Bruce Revesz
Stanley Rosenzwieg
Richard San Filippo
Kenneth Schermerhorn
Alan Silverman
James Simpson
Norman Smith
William Super
Scott Thornburg
James Tinsley
Jack Urban
Carleton Whelchel
Donald Whittaker
Alex Wilson
Wilmer Wise

TROMBONE

Norman Bernstein
Keith Brown
Douglas Edelman
Thomas Elliott
Paul Gay
Benjamin Herrington
Donald Hunsberger
John Kelly
Arthur Kerr
Fred Linge
Byron McCullough
Lee Margulies
John Mellick
Robert Moir
James Myrick
John Nickel
Benjamin Peck
George Powers
Allen Raph
Richard Rodda
Ralph Sauer
John Swallow
William Tesson
Scott Thornburgh
David Titcomb
Ray Turner
Joseph Williams

TUBA

Edmond Moore
Lewis Waldeck

Mischa Schneider.

TIMPANI AND PERCUSSION

Michael Bakan
Everett Beale
Allen Beard
Robert Becker
Joseph Beiro
Paul Berns
Charles Birch
Michael Bookspan
Frederick Buda
David L. Buttolph
William Cahn
Kalman Cherry
Nicholas D'Amico
Ron Delp
Gordon Emerson
Robin Engelman
Norman Fickett
Joseph Gramley
John Grimes
Neil Grover
Lee Gurst
William Hanley
Russell Hartenberger
Martha Hitchins
Matthew Hopkins
Ruth Jeanne
Jurij Konje
Morris Lang
David Mancini
Lloyd McCausland
Joseph Morrow
Andrew Power

James Priess
Linda Raymond
Leonard Schulman
Ellis Seamon
Stephen Silverman
Joel Thome
Luanne Warner
Don Williams
John Wyre

VOICE

Raoul Abdul
Jane Adler
Raquel Adonaylo
John Aler
Betty Allen
Carol Ann Allred
Theodore Paul Anderson
Miriam Barndt
Devy Barnett
Jenneke Barton
Inci Basarir
Bethany Beardslee
Herbert Beattie
Ara Berberian
Joan Bishop
Lawrence Bogue
Martha Bonta
Kathryn Bouleyn
Garnet Brooks
Patricia Brooks
Cyril Brosnan
Richard Brothers

Dorothea Brown
Janet Brown
Jenny Hayden Brown
Jules Bruyere
Gary Burgess
Mary Burgess
Henry Burroughs
Carol Carcieri
Walter Carringer
Marie Chavannes
John Cheek
Lawrence Chelsi
Katherine Ciesinski
David Clatworthy
Shirley Close
C. Evans Clough
Philip Cohen
Dorothy Cole
Donald Collup
Wayne Conner
Jesse Coston
Herbert Coursey
Charles Crook
Karen Crowley
Corinne Curry
Anne Dawson
Iona Delman
Sylvia Debenport
Carol Driggs
Martha Elliott
Mark Evans
David Evitts
Thomas Faracco
Constance Fee
Marthe Forget
Maureen Forrester
D'Anna Fortunato
Joseph Frank
Richard Frisch
Richard Fulton
Robert Galbraith
Nancy Gambuzza
Lillian Garabedian
Lin Garber
Marion Gedney
June Bonner Genovese
Phyllis Gieseler
Gary Glaze
Lillian Goldstein
Juliana Gondek
Otoniel Gonzaga
Lorie Gratis
Katherine Griffith
Victoria Grof
Leslie Guinn
Frank van Halsema
Carl Halvorson
Barry Hanner

Mary Ann Hart
Marty Hatch
Robert Hawthorne
Karen Louise Hendricks
Francis Hester
Patricia Hetkin
Joseph Himmel
Grayson Hirst
Diana Hoagland
Beverly Hoch
Linda Hohenfeld
Jane Holcomb
Gregory Hopkins
Anna Julia Hoyt
Jon Humphrey
Kate Hurney
Olga Iglesias
Angela Ingalls
Glendower Jones
Eleanor Kelley
Frank Kelley
Gary Kendall
John Kerr
Patricia Kirby Kerr
James King
Jasper King
Marlene Kleinman
Ilona Kombrink
Florence Kopleff
Walter Koppelman
Kim Kostenbader
Rosa Lamoreaux
John La Pierre
Timothy LeFebvre
Thomas Lewy
Suzanne Linden
Shirley Love
John Lundsten
Marcella Mace
John Magnuson
David Malis
Maria Martell
Grace-Lynn Martin
Marvis Martin
Glenda Maurice
Seth McCoy
Kevin McMillan
Joan Mey
Janice Meyerson
Beverly Morgan
Constantine Moskalenko
Nan Nall
Don Nelson
Mary Nessinger
Daisy Newman
Adelle Nicholson
Eva Nir
James Oleson

Kathleen Orr
Carol Page
Harold Parker
Elizabeth Patrick
Thomas Paul
Steffanie Pearce
Alexander Perkins
Janet Perry
Charlene Peterson
Robert Peterson
Susan Peterson
Ellen Phillips
Robert Phipps
Neva Pilgrim
Daniel Pincus
Anne Polen
Margaret Poyner
Glenn Priest
Elizabeth Pruett
Thomas Pyle
Ruth Ray
Isaac Reid
Georgine Resick
David Rice
Jennie Riesman
Jonathan Rigg

Michael Riley
Patrick Romano
Paul Rowe
Kathy Schuman
William Sharp
Kenneth Shelton
Lucy Shelton
Jerold Siena
Mary Simmons
Martial Singher
David Smith
Janet Smith
Karen Smith
André Solomon-Glover
Francesco Sorianello
Barbara Spangler
Margaret Stanback
Patricia Stasis
Herb Steiner
Katherine Stone
Sondra Stowe
Ellen Stuart
Shirley Sudock
Sanford Sylvan
Michael Sylvester
Ann Tatnall

Micheline Tessier
Gene Tucker
James Tyeska
Frederick Urrey
Benita Valente
Milagro Vargas
Claudia Visca
Eleanor Waddell
James Wainer
Margaretha Walk
Carol Werner
Mary Westbrook-Geha
Kimball Wheeler
John Paul White
John Wiseman
Ula Wolfe
Marvin Worden
William Workman
Gloria Wynder
William Yeats

VISITING AND RESIDENT COMPOSERS

John Adams
David Amram
Samuel Barber
Harold Boatrite
Elliott Carter
Paul Chihara
Aaron Copland
George Crumb
Luigi Dallapiccola
David Del Tredici
David Diamond
Lukas Foss
Alexander Heller
David Horne
Jeffrey Jones
Tonu Kalam
Earl Kim
Leon Kirchner
Barbara Kolb
Christopher Lantz
Fred Lerdahl
Philip Maneval
Marc Neikrug
George Perle
Walter Piston
Samuel Rhodes
Michael Riesman
Ned Rorem
Richard St. Clair
Gunther Schuller
Roger Sessions
Hsueh-Yung Shen
Seymour Shifrin
Rhys Scott

Robert Starer
Tison Street
Ivan Tcherepnin
Henry Weinberg
William Winstead

BACH CANTATAS

Blanche Honegger Moyse

BEETHOVEN CHORAL FANTASY

Pablo Casals
Felix Galimir
Tonu Kalam
Leon Kirchner
Seymour Lipkin
Alexander Schneider
Peter Serkin
Robert Shaw

SPECIAL CONTEMPORARY WORKS

Theodore Bloomfield
Leon Kirchner

OPERA WORKSHOP

Richard Aslanian
Carl Bamberger
Jack Benjamin
William Hughes
Martha Masséna
Philipp Naegele
Martial Singher
Michel Singher
Edwin Stahl
Felix Wolfes

REPERTOIRE AND RESEARCH COORDINATOR

Frederick Dorian

STRING REPERTOIRE

Mischa Schneider

WIND REPERTOIRE

Marcel Moyse

VOICE REPERTOIRE

Raquel Adonaylo

Blanche Moyse. FACING PAGE Julius Levine.

CREDITS

Photo and text selection and editing: J.M. Snyder

Design: Jackie Schuman

Production assistance: Philip Maneval, Kathy Schuman, Laura Clos

Special thanks to Shirley Ann Weekley, Peter Checchia, David White, Anthony P. Checchia and Frank Salomon for their additional assistance.

Special thanks to all of Marlboro's trustees and friends who contributed to Marlboro's 40th Anniversary Fund, which helped to underwrite the cost of this publication.

Photographs

Peter Checchia:
    p. 52 *(top)*, 53 *(bottom right)*, 55 *(top)*, 58 *(top)*, 66, 70, 72 *(top)*, 73 *(bottom)*, 80 *(left)*, 91 *(top left)*, 100 *(top)*, 106 *(top)*, 121 *(bottom)*, 123

Allen Cohen:
    p. 53 *(bottom left)*, 61, 79 *(top)*, 89

Paul Conklin:
    p. 17, 24 *(bottom)*, 25 *(top)*

George Dimock:
    p. 29 *(bottom)*, 30 *(top)*, 45 *(bottom)*, 49, 50 *(top and bottom right)*, 54, 59 *(top)*, 60, 64 *(top)*, 67 *(top)*, 68, 71, 72 *(bottom)*, 73 *(top)*, 75, 76, 78, 80 *(right)*, 86, 87, 99 *(top)*, 100 *(bottom)*, 102, 104, 105, 114, 115, 118, 121 *(top)*, 131

Boris Goldenberg:
    p. 16 *(top)*

Edward A. Hamilton:
    p. 23 *(top)*, 42, 48 *(top)*, 92 *(bottom left)*, 94 *(left)*, 95, back cover

George Harris:
    p. 13 *(bottom)*

©Clemens Kalischer:
    p. 5, 7 *(top)*, 8 *(top)*, 9, 10 *(bottom)*, 11 *(bottom)*, 12, 19, 21, 24 *(top)*, 32 *(bottom)*, 38 *(bottom)*, 41, 51, 62, 81 *(top)*, 82, 83, 84, 85, 91 *(top right)*, 111 *(top)*, 116

Ruth Laredo:
    p. 91 *(bottom)*, 130

Christoph Lehmann:
    p. 26, 36 *(right)*, 50 *(bottom left)*, 79 *(bottom)*, 133

Woodrow Leung:
    p. 27 *(top right)*, 28, 29 *(top)*, 30 *(bottom)*, 34, 35 *(bottom)*, 37, 45 *(top)*, 52 *(bottom)*, 59 *(bottom)*, 64 *(bottom)*, 65, 67 *(bottom)*, 74, 77, 81 *(bottom)*, 88, 97, 98, 99 *(bottom)*, 101 *(right)*, 103, 106 *(bottom)*, 117, 120, 129

©Rollie McKenna:
    p. 8 *(bottom)*, 11 *(top)*, 14, 122

©Lauren Piperno:
    p. 56, 57 *(bottom)*, 101 *(left)*

Fred Plaut:
    p. V *(bottom right)*, 3, 107 *(from the Fred and Rose Plaut Archives in the Yale Music Library)*

J.M. Snyder:
    p.15 *(top)*, 18, 25 *(bottom)*, 27 *(top left and bottom)*, 31, 40, 46, 57 *(top)*, 110, 112

Mitch Spencer:
    p. 132

Irene Strauss:
    p. 13 *(top)*

©Regina Touhey:
    p. 53 *(top)*, 55 *(bottom)*, 119

Vytas Valaitis:
    p. 38 *(top)*

Heinz H. Weissenstein/Whitestone Photo:
    p. 7 *(bottom)*, 15 *(bottom)*, 16 *(bottom)*, 22 *All rights reserved.*